Studies
on
Congress

Studies
on
Congress

Edited by

Sidney Wise

and

Richard F. Schier
FRANKLIN AND MARSHALL COLLEGE

Thomas Y. Crowell Company
New York · Established 1834

Preface

To the student who recalls that "all legislative powers" belong to Congress and that the American system neatly separates and divides powers, the immense complexities of the legislative process come as a disarming if not a disenchanting revelation. Understanding the constitutional role of Congress requires the realization that Congress is a bicameral maze of rules, customs, pressure points, interests, and personalities—all in the shadow of a President who so often appears to be guarding the nation's interests while individual legislators indulge their parochialism or vanities.

It is the purpose of this volume to compel the student to give each of these views a fresh, critical look by exposing him to some of the most sophisticated research and judgments offered on the Congress in recent years. Each selection deals with an issue of major concern. In addition, the arguments are presented in sufficient depth to allow for an understanding of the basis for the judgments reached by various scholars and political practitioners.

There is no single view of the Congress, and the authors included here diverge as to conclusions as well as to hypotheses. Former United States Senator Joseph S. Clark, long a proponent of congressional reform, describes the corporationlike atmosphere of the senatorial office that sought to serve twelve million Pennsylvania constituents while the Senator attempted to have some impact on public policy. Professor Ralph K. Huitt notes all of the irritating customs and rules of the Congress, yet he insists that ours is the most powerful and efficient national legislature in the world. The late Representative Clem Miller respectfully describes the pervasive intangibles of power in the House of Representatives,

v

a lesson available only from experience. Professor Charles O. Jones notes why the proposal that members of the House of Representatives be elected for four-year terms would have an extraordinary impact on our representative system. Paul W. Cherington and Ralph L. Gillen use a round-table discussion with nineteen Washington lobbyists to challenge many of the stereotypes about pressure group tactics. Professor Jeffrey L. Pressman, by studying the Appropriations Committees of the House and the Senate, illustrates how each committee inhabits a universe so distinct that the phrase "committee system" belies precision. Professor Lewis A. Froman, Jr., notes how distinctive constituencies can affect the voting records of Congressmen and why Senators are more likely than Representatives to respond positively to White House entreaties, party loyalties notwithstanding. And in words that are as timely today as when they were written in 1950, Professor Robert A. Dahl concedes the primacy of the President in the making of foreign policy, yet urges methods that will allow Congress a greater role in this critical area of responsibility.

While these topics merit the close study given by their distinguished authors, they hardly exhaust the range of issues and the rich scholarship presently available on the Congress. Hopefully the reader will regard these essays as reminders of how much there is to know before one can measure the significance of Congress as a maker of public policy.

Contents

CONTENTS

The Wonderful World of Congress

Joseph S. Clark

What the people as an entity expect of Congress as a body is at odds with what the constituent demands of the individual member of Congress. This is the lesson of the essay below by the former United States Senator from Pennsylvania, Joseph S. Clark.

We think of Congress as a legislative body, but as citizens (that is, voters) it is clear that we make demands on the members of Congress that seriously interfere with their capacity to function as legislators. But since tenure as a legislator is dependent on the continuing good will of the voters, the member of Congress finds that he must arrange his staff, his resources, and, above all, his own time to meet these demands. Being a representative of the people is clearly more than being their legislative agent and may, in some instances, conflict with the latter.

Clark sees the role of the member of Congress as consisting of two parts. First, there is the task of being a representative. In this role, the Senator or Congressman performs the function of

SOURCE: Joseph S. Clark, *Congress: The Sapless Branch* (New York: Harper & Row, 1964), ch. IV, pp. 51–79. Copyright © 1964 by Joseph S. Clark. Reprinted by permission of Harper & Row, Publishers.

humanizing government by mediating between it and the citizenry and assisting constituents with governmental problems. The second part of his duties concerns leadership, and in this capacity the member of Congress performs those tasks, principally legislative oversight of administration and participation in policy determination, that are commonly thought of as the major functions of Congress.

The difficulty is that in theory the second role is the important one for Congress, but realities all too often dictate that the first role is the truly important one for the individual member of Congress. This seems to suggest that the actual function of Congress dictated by political practice is different, or in danger of becoming different, from that assigned by constitutional theory. Those who look at Congress from without see it as a legislative body. Its members, however, view their role quite differently. An endless series of demands, most of them unrelated to the enactment of legislation, make huge inroads on the time available for legislative duties. Faced with a choice between an important meeting of a legislative committee or a civic occasion offering the opportunity to see and be seen by a thousand or so constituents, few members of Congress would hesitate—and even fewer would be at their place in the committee room.

The remedy that members of Congress have been required perforce to adopt in performing their legislative function is to specialize. They become experts on one or two complex matters, probably within the jurisdiction of their principal committee, and rely on the judgment of other members on matters outside their specialities. This remedy enables the Congress to function collectively as a legislative body, but it simultaneously circumscribes very narrowly the areas in which Senators or Representatives can exercise their leadership function. Willingness to defer to the judgment of others simplifies the passage of legislation of great complexity, but it does not arm the member of Congress with the technical virtuosity to educate his constituents or to withstand the pressures from either the congressional leadership or the White House.

"There is nothing self-evident about the proper role of Congress," writes Clark. The actual role of Congress seems dictated by the pressure of events. Its proper role, however, is more difficult to determine. Is it possible that Congress is not working as well as it should because individual members of Congress are working too hard at a role which is, in governmental terms, of lesser importance? The proper ordering of priorities may have to be the prelude to an effective Congress.

The election is over and won. For hundreds of members of Congress nothing very unusual has happened. They are the incumbents and the re-elected, who will be able to continue the work they are doing, and perhaps, with increased seniority in Congress, improve their committee assignments. If there has been a relatively large change of seats, as in the Democratic sweep of the Congressional elections of 1958, the chances of getting a different committee closer to one's heart or more important to one's district are naturally improved.

For newly elected members there are the tasks of moving families to Washington and setting up offices. Some members commute—mostly those members of the House known as the Tuesday-Thursday Club, Congressmen from the area near Washington, who remain in town for three days, usually at a hotel, and spend the rest of the time back in their districts. But most Congressmen bring their families to Washington and establish homes there. In view of the length of recent Congressional sessions, eight months and frequently more, it is necessary to do this if any appreciable time is to be spent with one's family. Indeed, for a good many members of Congress, Washington becomes home, their children go to school, they make friends and spend most of their time there. What used to be home becomes a retreat for weekends and holidays and headquarters for fence-mending trips around the district or state.

Whatever the arrangements, the Congressman must live in two places and travel back and forth between them a great deal. This imposes a heavy financial burden. It costs me money, quite a lot of my own money every year, to be a United States Senator. For those who have nothing in their pocket to take out, ways must be found to supplement the inadequate salary and expenses now paid members of Congress. Usually this means beating one's way along the "honorarium" trail picking up two hundred dollars here, five hundred there, to pay for the groceries and shoes for the kids.

Setting up an office, or several offices, is easier. Here the government is more generous (or the Congress is more sensible). The Congressman gets an office in Washington in one of the three House or two Senate office buildings—expensive, overadorned, inefficient buildings all of them. The two newest are, inexcusably, the most tasteless, poorly designed and expensive of them all. A Representative will get a suite of at least three rooms now that the Sam Rayburn House Office Building is completed (he used to get two). A Senator will get five or six rooms (he used to get three before the New S.O.B.—as it is known—was built several years ago). Committee chairmen and senior members of both houses get additional rooms, committee suites and hideaways in the Capitol itself.

The suites appear to be designed to impress the constituents or perhaps the member's ego; it is impossible to believe they were designed for genuine office use. The ceilings are high, the rooms deep, the woodwork massive and the furnishings Congressional (there is no other way to describe them). The member's personal office is usually lavishly enhanced by a marble fireplace in which you can't light a fire, a hidden wall safe that is rarely used, a refrigerator that is very useful indeed and private toilet facilities.

In the newer office buildings some thought has been given to built-in shelves and space for filing cabinets, but not much. And it is common to see the rather Edwardian elegance of the huge rooms in the Old Senate Office Building cut up and crisscrossed with ugly, homemade (in the carpentry shop in the basement) room dividers so that place can be found for the equipment, material and tools of work, and so that those on the staff who require it can have some semblance of privacy. It is typical that in my office the stationery must be stored in large, handsome, old-fashioned walnut bookcases with glass doors and curtains.

In addition, the Congressman may have an office or several offices right in his own district or state, usually in some federal building—a courthouse or post office, for example. These are rent-free and he gets an allowance to cover the housekeeping cost to the government of servicing them with heat, electricity, cleaning and so on. Because they are in ordinary federal buildings under the jurisdiction of the General Services Administration, these offices are a far cry from the Washington headquarters and are more likely to be shabby and underequipped.

The average House member has about six employees; it is normal to have four of them in the Washington office and two in the district. Of these, the two top aides usually do legislative and administrative staff work, and the remaining members of the staff do secretarial and clerical work. While there is an increasing tendency among Congressmen to have a high-caliber staff assistant doing full-time legislative work, many do their own legislative work or rely on committee staffs to advise them. In such cases—and they are numerous—the emphasis may be placed on an assistant whose principal forte is public relations or politics or both, since the two go hand in hand on the Hill. Almost inevitably, the other top assistant, sometimes female, is a combination office manager, government liaison worker, problem handler and greeter. These women, who swarm in the House of Representatives, are the mainstays of the offices. A freshman Congressman, if he is wise, finds or steals one to set up his office. For this is the woman who knows her way around in the complicated and illogical world of Congressional stationery offices, service departments, document rooms, who has mastered disbursing procedures and understands the importance of executive branch liaison. It is a bewildering and in some ways fantastic world, which would astonish the ordinary businessman and convulse a systems analyst.

In the district office, or offices, the Congressman may very well have a politician and secretary, though occasionally the order is reversed and most of the staff works out of the district office instead of Washington. Of the Pennsylvania delegation, only one House member chooses this latter course, though there are some who divide the personnel and the workload with equal emphasis on Washington and the district.

On the Senate side of the Hill the allowance for staff and equipment is much larger, and the Senatorial staff is therefore not only more numerous but more specialized. As a Senator from a large state I receive approximately $170,000 each year from the government for these purposes. Under a system so complicated as to be unintelligible, the larger states get more money, but not proportionately more, than the states with smaller populations.

There is an equally absurd and complicated system fixing staff salaries in arbitrary categories which must be adhered to. It was originally devised to conceal from the public the actual amount paid the employee. There is a covert quality about all this old-fashioned and illogical nonsense which makes the Congress appear petty and secretive. If there once was the excuse that these book-keeping procedures were nobody's business (neither the public's, the press's nor even the junior members of Congress's), that excuse was removed a few years ago when a diligent reporter began exposing these weird practices and brought sufficient public pressure to bear on Congress to make the facts available. The press and the public must still go to considerable trouble to obtain payroll information on Congressional salaries and positions, but for those who are interested enough to dig for it and diligent enough to study the rather obscure form in which the information is made available, it can be had.

All this might be quaint, and even amusing, were it unique—a relatively harmless example of a quill-pen tradition to remind us of the preautomated world. But it is not. The way Congress goes about its housekeeping chores is symptomatic of the deadly grip that traditions, customs and styles of the past have over the mentality of the nation's highest legislative body. For the new member of Congress, these details are his first glimpse of the special mystique and the peculiar malaise which have the Congress in thrall.

An even more important aspect of the neophyte's indoctrination into the ways of the Congressional world is the "word" he gets from those who run it. The late Sam Rayburn, Speaker of the House of Representatives longer than any man in history, gave each freshman class of Representatives the same advice for a generation: "To get along, go along." Speaker Rayburn's most illustrious protégé, President Lyndon Johnson, gave the same advice to newly elected Democratic Senators during his tenure as Majority Leader of the Senate. The Republicans heard, if not the same words, the same story. "To get along, go along" is the password to power on Capitol Hill.

Getting along and going along mean, for the first few months, being seen but not heard, doing your homework, watching out for your constituents, selecting the field of legislative interest which you intend to make your own and cooperating with the leadership of your party. That is what is expected of you.

When I arrived in Washington in 1957, I thought that my principal tasks for the next six years would be concerned with legislation. After the maelstrom of Philadelphia politics and four years of executive responsibility as Mayor, I looked forward enthusiastically to life as a national legislator. There would be time, I thought, to read, to listen, to think, to mull over problems, debate issues and to participate in framing wise laws.

But as so often happens, the world of the Senate was not what it appeared to be from outside the "hallowed chamber." The job of a member of Congress is a fascinating and rewarding one, but it is not what people generally think it is. Congress is not just the nation's legislature. Its job is not merely to pass new laws, amend or extend old ones and oversee executive administration. Perhaps its major business, at least in terms of time and energy expended, is to take care of the small but pressing needs of millions of American citizens.

Few people appreciate how large a part of the Congressman's day is spent not on grand affairs of state but on ministering to the inexhaustible requests of the people who elect him. His life is hardly one of splendid isolation, for his contacts with the world outside of Washington are continuous and time-consuming. He has too little time for sustained thought, for the demands upon him outmatch his capacity to meet them. Few Congressmen do many things which ought not to be done, but almost all of us leave undone things which ought to be done every day. Perhaps as a result, there is, in the words of the Book of Common Prayer, no health in us—miserable offenders that we are.

Senators are somewhat more insulated from constituent pressures than members of the House. Their larger staffs shield them from a good number of the demands that require the personal attention of a Representative. Yet members of both legislative bodies must devote a major part of their energies to constituent problems.

There are 5,673,497 registered voters in Pennsylvania out of a total population of some 11,500,000. My mail fluctuates from one thousand to ten thousand pieces a week. In an average year I receive fifteen thousand pieces of bulk mail (newspapers, magazines, reports, brochures, etc.) and 110,000 letters and postcards. Obviously, it would be physically impossible to read personally and answer any significant proportion of this flow. Much of it is repetitive, as when a lobby mounts a campaign to "snow" a legislator with pleas to enact or defeat a particular bill. Much of it requests assistance or information which can be answered adequately by staff. Some of it, alas, is full of hate and venom, signed and unsigned, printed and hand printed. A small part of it is crackpot, and another part is from schoolchildren who have been given the mistaken idea that their Congressman is a librarian. A colorful description of the mail has been given recently by Representative Clarence D. Long of Maryland:

A letter from PRAY (Paul Revere Association, Yeomen, Inc.) predicts that the nuclear test ban will end up with "the Russians and Zionists ruling the world, all Christianity wiped out, and all wives, mothers, and daughters in the brothels of Asia, China and India." George W. ("Wake up Humanity") Adams demands that I "banish organized religion damned quick lest organized religion banish the world a hell of a lot quicker." A neighbor wants to know, "What are you clowns doing in Washington?" A 13-year-old boy asks me if I have ever taken a bribe. A woman timidly seeks help in getting veterans benefits, since she just learned that her husband, who years ago abandoned her with 10 children, had recently died after living with another woman in Brazil.[1]

From time to time, people make demands that are so extreme that many of us have the desire to follow the example of former Congressman John Steven McGroarty of California, who wrote back to a constituent:

One of the countless drawbacks of being in Congress is that I am compelled to receive impertinent letters from a jackass like you in which you say I promised to have the Sierra Madre mountains reforested and I have been in Congress two months and haven't done it. Will you please take two running jumps and go to hell.[2]

Sometimes letters are remarkable in their senseless abuse, like the hate mail sent that fine Republican Senator, Thomas Kuchel of California, by members of the right-wing lunatic fringe, or the one sent by a citizen of Ohio to Senator Stephen Young. In a lengthy diatribe, the poison-pen artist viciously took to task, among others, welfare recipients, labor unions, the minimum wage, foreign aid, Chester Bowles, Nelson Rockefeller and Earl Warren. Young's reply was simple and to the point. "Dear Sir," the Senator wrote, "What else is new?" [3]

The volume of the mail, as well as the importance attached to it both by members of Congress and constituents, is what strikes the new legislator first, last and always. Of the twenty-five or so people on my staff, each and every one of them is concerned with the mail in one phase or another, half a dozen are preparing letters for my signature, and about a dozen spend their entire working day coping with it.

[1] Clarence D. Long, "Observations of a Freshman in Congress," *New York Times Magazine,* December 1, 1963.
[2] Quoted in John F. Kennedy, *Profiles in Courage* (New York: Harper & Brothers, 1956), p. 10.
[3] "The Reporter's Notes," *The Reporter,* August 16, 1962, p. 18.

As Mayor of Philadelphia I personally read, approved and signed almost everything that went out of my office over my signature. After one week in the Senate I made the administrative decision that since I would have to rely on the judgment of my staff to screen my mail for me, I would give them virtually complete responsibility for processing the mail and restrict my own mail-reading to what was obviously and absolutely necessary. This is the way it still works.

The mail is opened and sorted into categories. Volume mail on major issues, those on which fifty to a hundred letters come in every week, is answered by form letters on robotypers. Robo machines are semiautomated electric typewriters which will type a form letter at the press of a button. There is a newer, more expensive model which is fully automated. The robos will produce hundreds of perfectly typed letters in an afternoon; the superrobos will produce thousands of letters all night, while the staff and the Senator sleep! And the beauty of it is that only a real expert can tell a robotyped letter and signature from one personally dictated and signed.

These machines are used to cope with a large percentage of the mail, from half to two-thirds of it. The form letters used must be kept up to date as the legislation to which they pertain changes status in Congress or the problem to which they refer is resolved or dropped or forgotten. I rarely, if ever, write the form letter, but I do edit, change and then approve the draft prepared for me by the staff member most familiar with the subject and area of concern. Occasionally a letter I have personally dictated will be adapted or used as a robo form.

Additionally, dozens and dozens of so-called form letters (the distinction is almost meaningless nowadays) are prepared to answer mail which comes in dribs and drabs throughout the session —not enough, in other words, to warrant a mechanized operation. These are hand-typed by secretaries after they have been opened, read and marked in the mail process to designate their category: "education—pro"; "Bible reading—con"; "general views—for schoolchildren"; "Lithuanian Independence"; and so on. More than one hundred form letters are used in an average session of Congress, perhaps half of them prepared for "robo." These forms and "robos" are used to answer 80 to 90 percent of the mail.

That remaining 10 or 20 percent of the mail, however, takes as much or more time than all the rest put together. These are the letters which require individually prepared and hand-typed responses, as much because of who writes them as because of what they say. This mail is distributed among more than just professional or executive staff members, and may require more than just information or expertise. It may raise questions of policy or action to be taken; it may lead to a cable to the consul's office in Tegucigalpa or the drafting of new legislation; it may require a message of greeting or a picture and a biography. Whatever it requires or leads to, individual attention and time are necessary. Some of it is relatively routine and can be supervised and approved by my office manager. But a good deal of it is not routine and must be handled by those assistants, legislative and administrative, who work directly and fairly constantly with me, who thoroughly understand and can explicate my views, and who participate in the decision-making process. And while I can personally approve, and do, all form letters, I cannot take the time to read the hundreds of letters turned out each week by my top assistants. But I have perhaps the best staff on Capitol Hill and I trust its members implicitly. In seven years of dealing with my mail, they have never made a serious blunder and the minor mistakes could be counted on one's fingers. I am their willing captive.

In an average week I personally read and sign perhaps fifty letters.

How does the rest of the mail get signed? There is still another gadget widely used on the Hill for coping with this problem. I have one right in my own office, and it cost me $1,200 out of clerkhire—i.e., my office allotment.

My signature is reproduced, or forged if you will, to practically all my letters by a device known as an "autopen"—a wonderful product of automation which saves precious hours each week. There are three forged signatures. Most answers get the formal

"Joseph S. Clark." Politicians who are not intimate get "Joe Clark." Friends get "Joe," as do a fair number who are not friends but call me "Joe" when they write.

If this sounds disheartening to all those good people who write their Congressman, and want their views to be known to their Congressman, it is not meant to be, and should not.

First of all, the constituent's views are counted, noted and registered. I receive a monthly mail report informing me of the number of people who wrote and what they wrote about. I know that ten thousand Pennsylvanians wrote to me this year asking me to support federal aid to private schools, and the fact that I did not read each and every one of their letters does not make their position count for less. At the same time, the reply they received is an accurate account of my position on the subject of interest to them, very possibly in my own words. If I did not dictate the letter myself, the draft that was prepared for me in all likelihood included language I used in discussing this legislation in committee, or on the Senate floor, or in a speech, or in a staff meeting. Moreover, the staff members who have actually read the mail represent to me with objectivity and clarity the views and attitudes expressed in it on every issue under discussion. So in the end, the mail does what it is intended to do, and I make my decisions fully aware of that intention.

How much attention do I pay to my legislative mail? Some, but not much. It is useful as an indication of how certain groups of constituents feel, but to rely on it as an accurate guide to opinion would be folly. On the whole, mail is more trouble than it is worth as a reflection of public opinion. Public sentiment can be more accurately checked by reading the newspapers, talking or corresponding with political and leadership groups and conducting or following public opinion polls.

Many Senators and some Representatives follow the procedures respecting mail just outlined either from necessity, if they are from populous states or districts full of letter-writers, or, anyway, from a desire to save time for more important official duties.

Some Senators, particularly those from small states, and most

House members read all their mail and personally sign all the answers. Those who follow this procedure condemn themselves to devoting several hours each day to their correspondence.

Although comparatively few citizens, out of a staggering potential in a large district or state, come to see their Representative or Senator, many do—particularly if they live fairly close by. There are always more visitors seeking to shake hands or chat with their Congressman than he can possibly find time to see. Especially during vacation periods, whole families flock to Washington, swarming through the Capitol and calling legislators off the floor of the two chambers or "just dropping in" at the office to be recognized by the men who represent them on Capitol Hill.

Despite the time factor, the effects of face-to-face meetings with constituents are often rewarding. There is real satisfaction in discussing current issues such as disarmament, Congressional reform or educational needs with the student and civic groups that visit with me. It often clarifies thinking to talk with Pennsylvania businessmen and labor leaders about issues with which they are concerned. There are also, however, the daily instances of being collared by constituents whose chief purpose is to say "Hello," usually with the added good news that they voted for me and I haven't done anything for them lately.

The difficulty is that there are only twenty-four hours in a day. As a result of these persistent demands from one's constituency, the Congressman has become in large part a delegate responsible for rendering personal service. One former member of the House expressed this aspect of the Congressman's role accurately when he said:

A Congressman has become an expanded messenger boy, an employment agency, getter-out of the Navy, Army, and Marines, a wardheeler, a wound healer, trouble shooter, law explainer, bill finder, issue translator, resolution interpreter, controversy-oil-pourer, glad hand extender, business promoter, veterans affairs adjuster, ex-serviceman's champion, watchdog for the underdog, sympathizer for the upperdog, kisser of babies, recoverer of lost baggage, soberer of delegates, adjuster for traffic violations and voters straying into the toils of the law, binderup of broken hearts, financial wet nurse, a good samaritan, contributor to good causes, cornerstone layer, public building and bridge dedicator and ship christener.[4]

Here again the staff is helpful, both as a screen and as properly trained and qualified representatives of the member himself. The visitor whose primary purpose is to meet or greet the Congressman may very well be disappointed if he doesn't get to see him "in person." But those who want something done can usually be satisfied with efficient and courteous treatment from a staff expert experienced in dealing with such problems. A surprising number of people drop by my office just to get passes for the House and Senate gallery, or tourist information, or just to touch base with their home-state Senator without asking or expecting to see me or anyone else. They sometimes leave notes. More frequently they tell my receptionist to "just say hello." But there are always enough visitors, singly and in groups, to keep me busy greeting people all day long if I chose to do so.

The choice varies among members of Congress. A few may see all visitors, even take many of them to lunch or on personally conducted tours of the Capitol. Most see as many as they feel they can. A few Senators—Paul Douglas and Hubert Humphrey among them —have given themselves a daily quota which they usually meet.

The reason a Congressman spends so much time on these routine tasks is largely that he is gregarious and also that he is a politician. The Congressman thinks, with good reason, that proper performance in his contacts with constituents will help him win re-election. The birthday and condolence letters to constituents, the copies of the government publication, *Child Care,* that are sent to new mothers, the research materials that are mailed to high school students, the endless congratulatory notes to those who distinguish themselves back home, all constitute part of a continuous selling job. The Congressman is always trying to impress upon his electorate not only his name, which is more difficult than may appear at first

[4] Luther Patrick, "What Is a Congressman?" reprinted in *Congressional Record,* May 13, 1963, daily ed., p. A2978.

glance, but also the idea that he is faithfully servicing their individual needs and forwarding their individual aspirations. The better these jobs are carried out, the more leeway he has when it comes to the business of legislation.

While a Congressman is rarely called upon to give advice to the lovelorn, it is extraordinary how often he acts as a father confessor to his constituents. "Please listen to my story and tell me what to do" comes in the mail every day and over the phone several times a week, and often in the evening or over the weekend when one is trying to get away from it all for a little relaxation or sleep.

Some of the personal services are vital to the citizen who suffers injustice or undue delay at the hands of the executive bureaucracy. Rules and procedures of executive departments lead to injustices to individuals more frequently than one might think. Here the Congressman or his staff must intervene in an effort to humanize what is inevitably a hardened bureaucratic process.

A goodly portion of the work that comes to my offices consists of "cases," requests for a wide variety of services requiring me to go to bat for citizens with the administrative agencies of the federal government. Not all the requests are valid, but many are.

The very knowledge by executive officials that some Congressman is sure to look into a matter affecting his constituents acts as a healthy check against bureaucratic indifference or arrogance. Congress performs a useful function in acting as errand boy, correspondent and father confessor.

The mail and the visitors have to fit into a schedule. And so do a good many other things. Here is Congressman Long's description of this schedule:

My "rubber-chicken" calendar for a not untypical week included the following: Addressed students of three high schools visiting the House floor, veterans groups from two counties, officers club in Army Chemical Center, and civil-defense officials of seven states; attended meeting of 13th District Community Council, and various meetings on urban renewal, alcoholism, and relocation of a post office; attended a bar mitzvah, two bull roasts, and dedication of a school; went to a

Democratic club dinner, a political cocktail party and dinner for a visiting Indian industrialist.

This routine—on top of legislative and administrative work—goes on seven days and five nights a week, except in July and August. Holidays are busiest. On July 4, I marched in four parades, smiled at 200,000 people, spoke to 5,000 more in the evening, attended a party, drove 100 miles.[5]

My own typical schedule for one day would go something like this:

Up by seven, skim the *Congressional Record,* read the Washington *Post,* breakfast, off to work by eight, walking the first mile, then picking up my secretary and a cab, reading *New York Times* and sometimes dictating a letter or two en route; arrive at office 8:30, read Philadelphia *Inquirer*; read testimony to be presented at ten-o'clock committee hearing or start on "incoming" box; go over day's schedule with secretary; staff meeting at 9:00, giving assignments, hearing reports, discussing advance schedule for speeches, appearances, etc.; committee meeting 10:00–12:00, sometimes shuttling back and forth between two, occasionally three, committee hearings scheduled simultaneously; lunch with journalist, official of executive branch, members of Congress, staff, constituents, or—rarely—family and friends; check Senate floor, perhaps insertion in record or brief "morning hour" remarks, put name on list for speech later in day, talk with other Senators and Majority Leader about various problems and pending legislation; thirty-minute rest or nap; seclusion in private Capitol office (first obtained through seniority in 1963) to read reports, memos, studies, or perhaps to write; to Senate floor to participate in debate, offer amendments, make speech; radio or television program or press interviews; return to Senate Office Building office around 5:00 for desk and paper work, individual meetings with staff members, visitors, Pennsylvania politicians until 6:30; home to bathe and change for dinner, perhaps at home but more likely with my wife at an embassy, a colleague's, an official function, a Cabinet officer's or, occasionally, just a friend's;

[5] Long, *op. cit.*

where in each case almost always I pick up something worth knowing and meet under informal circumstances people who contribute to my education. Weekends are frequently interrupted by politics, speeches, visits from constituents; but we keep a good part of them to ourselves for tennis, reading, writing and fun with friends.

During the course of the day I will have received a hundred phone calls, ten of which I may have picked up; phoned my secretary and administrative and legislative assistants from the Capitol several times each; talked to my Philadelphia office; and talked with my wife to check on our engagements and schedule.

Almost every Friday afternoon, we go back to Philadelphia by train in time for dinner, getting some paper work done en route. Most Monday mornings I come back to Washington on the morning Congressional, arriving at the office at 10:30. But if there is a committee meeting or early Monday morning appointment, I get up at 6:30, take a commuter train to Thirtieth Street Station, then a taxi to the airport for a plane that gets me to the office by 9:00.

All of this takes time—lots of time. Where does the member of Congress find it—even enough time to do a small part of all this?

The answer is that he has to. He must order his life with rigorous self-discipline. And he must hire the best staff he can get on the rather generous allowances given to him for this purpose and then delegate every nonessential and many fairly important duties to his qualified assistants instead of trying to do it all himself. When he has accomplished this task, he should be well on the way to becoming an effective Representative or Senator.

In a recently published study of the Congress, Charles L. Clapp notes the common complaint of Congressmen that they lack time to perform their job, especially the legislative functions, which should constitute their primary responsibility.[6]

The difficulty of the time factor is compounded by the widely held belief that legislative work is not particularly noticed or appreciated by the constituents, and that it does less to help the Con-

---

[6] Charles L. Clapp, *The Congressman—His Work as He Sees It* (Washington, D.C.: The Brookings Institution, December, 1963), p. 104.

gressman get re-elected than "bringing home the bacon"—providing service to constituents—and good public relations.

This is perhaps less true of the Senate than the House, but it is all too true. Yet the legislative work must be done, and it becomes more complex and more crucial with each passing year. The way out of this dilemma for most Congressmen is to seek refuge in specialization, to place heavy reliance on the committee system, and to go along with the recommendations of senior colleagues or the leadership on matters on which he is not an expert.

In the House some members get two major committee assignments, more only one. In the Senate each Senator gets at least two legislative committee assignments, and sometimes three or four major ones.

After he gets his committee assignment (and he may be lucky enough or smart enough—i.e., play his cards right with the ruling clique—to get the committee of his first choice, his first term), the Congressman is encouraged by his chairman and senior colleagues to select one or two aspects of the committee's work in which to become expert. Then, as Clapp puts it:

The emphasis on specialization simplifies significantly the task of the representative. Colleagues turn to him for aid in determining their own position on legislative matters which arise within his field of competence; he, in turn, settles on one or two trusted colleagues on each committee to whom he can turn for clarification or advice regarding proposals falling within their committee's jurisdiction.[7]

Useful, and even necessary, as this may be, the practice has some questionable consequences. In matters vital to the national interest, including defense, the vast majority of Congressmen must rely on the judgment of a handful of other members without really understanding how or why those judgments were made. Here is the observation of a House member on the subject:

This matter of the budget, especially the defense budget, and the whole area of executive oversight is a very difficult one. . . . There

[7] *Ibid.*, p. 111.

is a tendency for the average member to throw up his hands in handling such matters. There is also a haunting fear if we vote to cut certain phases of the program we may be hampering national defense.[8]

Despite the endless pieties in Congress about balancing the budget and cutting expenditures, the Defense budget—the single biggest expenditure in the world, by our or any other government —sails through Congress with very little trouble and less floor discussion, much as the executive branch requests it. In the Senate in 1963 it was passed in two hours. In fact, in recent years, the executive branch has had to refuse to spend enormous sums added to the budget by Congress—for nuclear carriers and nuclear planes —which the Secretary of Defense and the President didn't even want.

"Congress in its committee rooms is Congress at work," Woodrow Wilson wrote, in 1885, and this statement is more true today than it was then. It is in the committee room that the Congressman spends a good deal of his time, and there the real legislative work is done.

Thousands of bills are introduced each session. Some Representatives introduce a great many; some introduce none. The fact that he introduces a bill does not necessarily mean the Representative is committed to it; he may be doing it at the request of constituents, an interest group or the executive branch of the government. On the other hand, under the House system a member will often introduce a bill identical to one already introduced by another, particularly if it is a major administration legislative program—an education bill or a civil rights bill—to demonstrate his support for the legislation. Thus a hundred identical bills may be introduced in the House. In the Senate members are permitted to cosponsor each other's bills to avoid duplication. Many bills introduced in the Senate will have ten, twenty or even fifty cosponsors from both sides of the aisle.

All bills are referred to the appropriate legislative committee— that is, the committee having jurisdiction over the area covered by

[8] *Ibid.*

the bill. There are sometimes jurisdictional disputes, and a bill may then have to pass through more than one committee before passage. In addition, after passage, an appropriation must often be obtained before its provisions can become effective. The Communications Satellite bill, for example, went to the Commerce, Space, and Foreign Relations Committees. Thereafter the Appropriations Committees had to agree on the amount to be expended.

Most of the bills on which the committees actually hold hearings are those sent down to the Hill by the administration, those introduced by the chairman of the committee, those introduced by senior ranking members and those sponsored by a large number of members. Occasionally an individual Senator's bill may become law, as when he fathers the idea for a brand-new program or concept such as the Fulbright Scholarship Program, but this does not happen very often.

When I ran for the Senate the first time, I took a look at my incumbent opponent's record and saw that no legislation of any importance bore his name. I went up hill and down dale in Pennsylvania calling this dereliction of duty to the attention of the people of Pennsylvania. And while I was able to get my name on some rather important legislation in my first term in the Senate, I am not sure, knowing what I know now, that I should have said what I did say during that campaign.

I spend more hours in committee meetings than I do on the floor of the Senate. So does everyone else. In the House, where the rules for floor procedure leave little time for debate on legislation, the Congressman can do little more than vote yes or no on the legislation. The House has a rule limiting debate on amendments to five minutes; total time of debate is often limited by the Rules Committee. In the Senate, where unlimited debate prevails, the individual Senators can offer as many amendments as they wish and obtain roll-call votes on them.

When the two houses have passed bills on the same subject which are not identical, meetings are held by representatives of both parties in each House, known as Conference Committees, to iron out the differences in the bills and report an agreed version back to the two houses—or, occasionally, to report that they can't agree. These final steps of the legislative process are very important. Conference Committees are sometimes referred to as the "third house," for while they cannot initiate proposals contained in either the House or Senate versions of the legislation they frequently agree to a compromise which bears little relation to either bill sent to conference.

In 1946, as a part of the Congressional Reorganization Act, Congress passed the Regulation of Lobbying Title requiring the registration of those who seek to influence legislation. By 1963, some 6,500 lobbyists had so registered. This is a rough index of the pluralistic nature of our society. Some of these names, of course, represent duplication. Still others represent organizations whose concerns are quite narrow. A very large number, however, maintain constant vigilance over not only that part of the work of Congress which concerns them but, with varying degrees of concern, most of the major bills.

There was a time when the economy of Pennsylvania meant coal, steel, railroads and farms, and the task of a Senator from the Commonwealth was primarily to concern himself with their well-being. Long before the lobbies were registered these "interests" were amply represented in Washington. But now the economy of Pennsylvania has become so complex and diversified that so simplistic a conception of Senatorial duties is no longer possible. And this is true of most other states in the Union, small as well as large.

The member of Congress, as part of his extra-legislative duties, must serve as a kind of lobbyist himself—a connecting link between government and a wide variety of delegations, groups and interests that have influence in his state or district. In one respect, this is just good politics, but in a more inclusive sense it is one of the reasons why the Congressman is in Washington. Although he cannot always give complete satisfaction and although he sometimes gets annoyed by intemperate demands from vested interests with political muscle back home, he must always be available, ready to lend an attentive ear to almost any problem.

Naturally, delegations visit with me, talk about their problems and suggest how I might help. The result is nearly always to teach me something important and new. In May, 1963, for example, I lunched with Pennsylvania shoe manufacturers, who complained, with some justice, about foreign competition. The next day I was descended upon by a delegation of machinists from a York union, who wanted the government to purchase hydroelectric turbines from their employer to insure their continued employment. Several days later I met delegates of the Pennsylvania Chamber of Commerce, who were unhappy about the small number of defense contracts in the state.

The following week, after requests from city officials and civic groups, I introduced a bill in the Senate to authorize a World's Fair in Philadelphia in 1976 and made, I suspect, a somewhat corny speech in its behalf.

Valuable time and energy, which might otherwise be devoted to legislation, is spent by both the Congressman and his staff in taking care of this flood of organized constituent requests. Yet rarely are the demands of the lobbies entirely unreasonable. Usually, they present a point of view which should be considered in making up one's mind how to act. When the demand is unreasonable, it is more often based on ignorance of the countervailing arguments than on an arbitrary insistence on a point of view known to be untenable.

The word "lobby" has an unnecessarily evil connotation. It is true that some pressure groups "put the arm" on a Congressman, particularly if they have supported him during his campaigns. It is also true that occasionally a lobbyist attempts to wine and dine a Congressman whose support is needed. Certain Congressmen are known as being willing "clients" of the military, of defense contractors, of the AFL-CIO or of the U.S. Chamber of Commerce. The airlines, the railroads, the railroad brotherhoods, the highway lobby, among many others, are active indeed in Washington. But on the whole the direct influence of lobbies on the Congress is not so great as on the average state legislature. While an individual Congressman here and there may be a virtual spokesman for a lobby's point of view, this may be due as much to ideological coincidence as to any dirty work afoot.

This is not to say that lobbies cannot be influential. They can be, but usually they achieve what they want as one part or aspect of a tide or movement that includes a great many people. For example, the savings and loan institutions wanted a change in the House-passed tax bill of 1961 to eliminate the withholding tax on interest, and they got the change they wanted; but they also had the support of a vast—and misleading—newspaper campaign which brought over sixty thousand letters to my office in support of their position. I voted against eliminating the provision anyway, but most Senators, who had received a proportionate amount of similar mail, did not. They did so not because the savings and loan lobby was for the change, but because so many of their constituents seemed to be also.

There is no doubt that many of the lobbies had made influential friends in high places. But the Congress is too large, unwieldy and diverse to be pushed around often even by a very powerful single interest. There are a few rotten apples in the Congressional barrel, as there are everywhere else; but influence-peddling in government, despite the disclosures of the Bobby Baker case, has been overrated. I do not defend either the lobbies or any of my colleagues for behavior which may be unethical and is certainly sometimes irresponsible, but the relationship between a member of Congress and a lobby—from a lunch to a campaign contribution—is, more often than not, perfectly aboveboard and legitimate.

Most of the larger and well-organized lobbies have legislative staffs, of their own, including in many cases excellent lawyers, well-trained economists, statisticians and the like. It is safe to say that the AFL-CIO and the Teamsters' International know more about a complicated piece of labor legislation than the committee members who worked on and drafted the bill; and that the American Medical Association lobbyists know as much about all the different legislative approaches to the problem of health care for the aged as the White House staff.

In this, the lobbyists serve a particularly useful function. Their fine-tooth-comb study of a bill may reveal "sleepers" in the legislation of which most members have not been aware, or about which they did not understand the far-reaching and long-range implications.

When a committee chairman reports to the floor a hundred-page housing bill or a 175-page tax bill, the average Congressman will not undertake to study every line of the bill. The interested and affected lobbies will, however, and the axes they have to grind will bring to the surface issues helpful both to those who wish to support their position and those who oppose it.

In sum, the lobbies perform a useful educational function for most Congressmen. But like other experts they should be kept on tap and not on top.

A positive responsibility of Congress as an institution and of Congressmen as individuals is to keep the general public informed about the business of the nation. This duty applies to the country at large for the institution and to his own constituents for the individual Congressman. It is performed in many ways.

The legislative functions of Congress have important educational aspects. So does the oversight function, of which more hereafter. The publicity attendant on the introduction of a bill, the public hearings before committees both legislative and investigatory, committee reports, floor debate and the daily publication of the *Congressional Record* are all methods by which Congress, the institution, keeps the public informed.

So long as the educational work of the institution is done in committee it is done fairly well. There are exceptions where committee members browbeat witnesses, where witnesses drone on with little to contribute, where reports are badly prepared, where, in the case of investigations, one wonders why they were ever started. But on the whole a Congressional hearing or committee report is a mine of useful information to those who seek to be informed.

The late Senator Estes Kefauver's reputation was made and will long survive in history for his educational efforts. He was the first to turn the spotlight on the connections between interstate and in-

THE WONDERFUL WORLD OF CONGRESS   **25**

ternational gangsters and crooked local politicians. Through his efforts a score of law enforcement agencies bestirred themselves and sent a hundred crooks to jail. The efforts of the Anti-monopoly Subcommittee of the Judiciary Committee of the Senate, which he chaired, was responsible for more vigorous prosecution of the antitrust laws, including the conviction of top officials of the General Electric Company, Westinghouse and others for conspiring to fix prices. It also collected the data necessary to push to passage the Drug Act of 1962 after the country became aroused over the Thalidomide scandal.

Senator Henry Jackson's Subcommittee on National Security Organization has made a valuable contribution. So have Senator Humphrey's Subcommittee on Disarmament, Senator Paul Douglas' hearings on the Truth in Lending Bill, Senator Eugene McCarthy's Special Committee on Unemployment of 1959–60, and Senator Pat McNamara's Special Committee on Problems of the Aging.

The Joint Economic Committee annually conducts educational hearings on the various matters raised by the President's Economic Report under the alternative chairmanship of Senator Douglas and Congressman Wright Patman of Texas.

On the House side, the Subcommittee on Government Information chaired by Representative John Moss of California has made a useful contribution through hearings on the knotty problem of how far the public's "right to know" extends as against the need for keeping secret information which might aid a potential enemy.

While some of these Congressional hearings are conducted on specific bills and are intended as a preliminary to direct legislative action, most of them are not. Their primary purpose is educational, i.e., to inform the public of conditions which exist in the hope that efforts to remedy abuses will result.

But the wearisome and irrelevant talk on the floor of the Senate contributes little to the job of education. Few qualified observers refer to the Senate today as "the greatest deliberative body in the world" without a twinkle in the eye. And while the House has a strictly enforced rule of germaneness and a time limitation on speeches, there are few dedicated readers of the record of its proceedings. In fact, there are those who consider the *Congressional Record* one of our more comic magazines.

This is not to say that debate does not sometimes rise to high levels, particularly in the short, sharp clash of minds in colloquy just before a controversial bill goes to the vote. It does. But these occasions are small oases in a desert of tediousness.

The educational function of the individual Congressman is different. In order to educate, he must communicate off the floor and out of committee. One difficulty with some Congressmen, it must be admitted, is that they often attempt to communicate when they have nothing to say. This has resulted in those devastating reprints from the *Congressional Record* appearing from time to time in *The New Yorker* under the heading "Wind on Capitol Hill." It has also made the Congressman the butt of many a cartoon, Lichty's "Senator Snort" being the prototype.

All Congressmen will periodically have a message they want to get across to the voters back home. There are a number of ways of doing this. Correspondence, newsletters, speeches on and off the floor, press releases, radio and television broadcasts are the media every Congressman uses. And occasions frequently will arise where reporters will seek out a Congressman to elicit his views on a particular subject on which he is thought to have some special competence.

It is a rare Congressman who is not anxious to have his thoughts and actions reported in all areas of the communications media. All things considered, the coverage is good; yet there are conspicuous failings. Nobody has stated them better than the late Clem Miller, until his death Representative from the First California District, in his newsletters, published in 1962 under the title *Member of the House*.[9]

Congressman Miller pointed out that major stories are sometimes not covered at all. For example, on one occasion the chairman of

[9] Clem Miller, *Member of the House; Letters of a Congressman* (New York: Scribner's, 1962), pp. 59–62.

the House Rules Committee tried to chastise a Congressman for being critical of him on a radio broadcast. As a result, the subsurface feud between Northern Democrats and the Rules Committee broke into the open. The incident might well have been heralded as an historic turning point in the development of the House. "Yet," Mr. Miller wrote, "there was not a line, *not a line,* of this 'effort to censure' in the newspaper the following day. A complete blackout. . . . So concerned is the press with the surface events of the day that the meaning of life in Washington is many times all but obscured or actually distorted beyond resemblance."

The dilemma of the Congressman is obvious. "If the press did not report Congress," Mr. Miller said, "Congress could hardly function. If the sound of congressional voices carried no farther than the bare walls of the Chambers, Congress could disband. We know this; it is brought home to us every day. Reporters appear very aware of their powers. . . . This suggests a basic rivalry between the press corps and Congressmen."

One difficulty is that, since the press operates under the constant pressure of meeting a deadline, the reporters are tempted to think in clichés and to write slogans. Therefore they prefer to have Congressmen do likewise. The press, as a rule, has no time to listen or discuss and, on occasion, not even the time to think. The result is an inevitable distortion that comes from oversimplification and compression. Moreover, most of the trouble is not with the reporters. It is with the editors and publishers back home. Too often they reflect an ill-informed attitude toward national affairs. Too often they present biased news coverage because their editorial policy is partisan. The pernicious influence, conscious and subconscious, of advertisers on editors and broadcasters may also be a real evil.

The wide variety of ability and performance of both reporters and the publications they work for should be stressed. They range all the way from superlatively good to pretty pathetic. An astute Congressman will promote his relations with the former and hope the latter will let him alone.

However good the press coverage in Washington may be, the

important thing to the member of Congress is what gets printed and reported on TV and radio back home in his district. Copy that is written and filed but never appears is not much help. Most members of Congress, therefore, establish direct contact with the papers in their district, phoning and wiring news of contracts, postmaster nominations, awards, hospital grants and so on. This purely local news will receive more play in the local press, particularly the smaller papers and the weekly press, than some major statement of policy on a grave national issue. I have made long speeches in the Senate on disarmament, civil rights and the manpower revolution which inspired either a few paragraphs from the wire services or nothing at all in many a paper with less than 25,000 circulation in Pennsylvania. But when I have forwarded the announcement of a new post office or a million-dollar contract award, I have been blessed with streamer headlines, even pictures, and once a special box on the front page of the Pottstown *Mercury* headed, "Thank You, Senator!" And, usually, I had little, if anything, to do with the award.

Many Congressmen write newsletters to their constituents which are released to the press and appear as a regular column in local papers, again primarily in weeklies and smaller papers.

Press releases—the well-known Washington handout—are legion from all offices in the Capitol, and while the metropolitan press and individual reporters may look down on them, or consider them worth only a paragraph or two, many papers will print them, especially if they favor the member's politics. Because of the time factor, the press release is not much good for spot news, but can be useful for a weekend story and as background for future stories on the same subject.

There is a radio and TV gallery just above the chamber floor in both houses where tapes are made for later broadcast. The Congressman interested in his educational role, or his administrative assistant acting on his behalf, will solicit opportunities to use the gallery when he has something worth saying. And outside the doors of each chamber lurk daily the portable-tape-recording radio reporters anxious for anything, or almost anything, a Congressman wants to say in one minute about issues pending in committee or on the floor. This is sold as spot news for the local stations back home on a syndicated basis outside the network systems. The Congressman will do well to patronize them.

For radio and TV most members of Congress also provide, as with the newsletter, special services of their own, most often regularly produced programs or reports to be carried on local radio and television stations. There are TV and radio studios in the basement of both the House and the Senate where for a nominal charge tapes can be cut and mailed home. Since 1959 my Republican Senatorial colleague, Hugh Scott, and I have, every two weeks during the session, appeared on a half-hour TV program, "Your Senators' Report," to the people of Pennsylvania. For political reasons we are off the air whenever one of us is up for re-election.

Senator Scott and I believe the program has a dual value. It helps educate our constituents in the issues and controversies of the day, and it gives a platform from which to enunciate our respective party and personal positions on those issues. We believe it helps us as Senators to play a positive role in national affairs.

There are, then, innumerable ways in which a Congressman can utilize the media of communications both to educate his constituents and, in that ghastly Madison Avenue phrase, "project his image." The media are not perfect. But they are very good. How skillfully a Congressman uses them will have a real bearing not only on his chances of surviving but on the contribution he will make to the public performance of the United States Congress.

There is nothing self-evident about the proper role of Congress. But it is clearly high time that the Congress makes the effort to figure out what it is doing. Perhaps its representative function has been carried out in the best possible manner. Certainly as a personal representative of his constituents, a mediator between governmental bureaucracy and the rank-and-file citizen, a case worker or errand boy for the folks in his state or district, the Congressman today performs indispensable service. And it is service that cannot be done by any other agency of the federal government.[10]

As an educator and leader of his constituents the performance is spottier. Some do, some don't perform the task well. But when we deal with Congress in its relationships with the executive there is real difficulty. The problems here are twofold: first, how can Congress keep a watchful eye on the operating conduct of the executive departments and agencies without interfering in day-to-day administration and without usurping executive functions; and second, how can Congress responsibly participate in the formulation and consideration of national policy?

Congressmen must wear two somewhat different sets of lenses in viewing their responsibilities. They have to look to their states or districts, since they have the duty of representing the people back home. But they have also to look to the nation and its needs, which are not always identical with the sum of the needs of the separate states and districts. In this second capacity, they must work hand in hand with policy makers in the executive branch, enacting legislation and checking on its administration, in the interests not of diverse and separate constituencies but rather of the general public.

[10] Representative Henry S. Reuss has recently suggested that we institute a new type of Administrative Counsel who would handle many of the service functions of Congressmen. The Ombudsman, as he is called in the Scandinavian countries, deals primarily with constituent problems with the bureaucracy, thus allowing Members to spend more time on the study of legislation. See *Congressional Record,* July 16, 1963 (daily ed.), p. 12067.

Congress, the Durable Partner

Ralph K. Huitt

The constitutional separation of powers in America has produced separate institutions of government, writes Mr. Huitt, and these institutions, in turn, profoundly influence the behavior of their members. Members of Congress act differently than members, say, of the bureaucracy because these distinct institutions demand and expect different kinds of behavior from those who function within them.

With this as his central premise, Mr. Huitt suggests that our understanding of Congress might be built upon comparative research into legislatures. All legislative bodies perform several functions besides that of legislation (for example, oversight of the executive), and it may well be that they accordingly influence the behavior of their members in similar ways.

Mr. Huitt is here arguing that Congress be studied in relation to other legislative bodies in other political systems, and he suggests a number of provocative questions to which answers might

SOURCE: Elke Frank, ed., *Lawmakers in a Changing World* (Englewood Cliffs, N.J.: Prentice-Hall, 1966), pp. 9–28. © 1966. Reprinted by permission of Prentice-Hall, Inc.

be sought and hypotheses which are deserving of exploration. Congress is to be seen, at least in part, as a separate institution rather than as a segment of a larger political system. Analysis of the functioning of Congress is to be directed along the lines of comparative legislative development rather than as an evolutionary aspect of the American political system. In his words, "the influence of an institution in all its historic dimensions may be stronger than those which are products of a peculiar national experience."

There can be scarcely any question that this might be a most fruitful line of inquiry. Studies of Congress have tended to be internal, that is, of the committee structure or leadership structure, or they have related the functioning of Congress to other elements, notably, of course, the Presidency, in the American system of government. From these studies have emerged our understanding of congressional behavior, the familiar litany of criticisms of Congress, and the perhaps even more familiar catalogue of proposed reforms.

Congress, it is frequently said, can be obstructive only in its legislative capacity. It lags behind the Executive in its response to events, partly because its constituency is different and partly because it first fractionalizes and then concentrates power internally among its least responsive elements. Thus, frustrated in its desire to play a creative role in social change, Congress vents its frustration by seeking to reassert, through policing the administration of laws, powers which it can no longer assert at the inception of those laws.

This seems a fair summary of the recent literature on Congress. The conversion of Congress into "the sapless branch," to use former Senator Clark's phrase, is a recurrent theme. But is the Congress at present, whether as pictured or caricatured above, a creation of events within American society and the American political process? Or is Congress the way it is because of the institutional response to be expected from a legislative body confronting roughly similar developments in a roughly similar environment?

The answers to these questions are of crucial importance. Change or adaptation of Congress, in any conscious sense, requires an accurate diagnosis of the source of present behavior.

Alteration or reform of the Congress in any institutional way cannot be neutral. Change of any significance will in the most fundamental sense affect the distribution of power in our governmental system. It takes no prescience to suggest that in the next few years our system of government will face unprecedented challenges in managing the emergent conflicts of our society. Consideration of the place of Congress in this task needs to be set against the broader background of the role of the legislative assembly in modern, pluralistic societies.

It is ironic that the representative assembly, whose great historic achievement was the taming of the executive, is now almost everywhere submissive once more to him and his establishment. The notable exception among national legislatures is the Congress of the United States. Congress cannot match the drama of the presidency but any day it sits it can remind the executive that it must be taken into account. Its leaders are men of political substance and its members can, even in their individual capacities, influence public policy. My purposes are to state briefly some reasons why Congress has maintained its place in the constitutional partnership, to consider some of the factors which affect that partnership, and to suggest some lines of inquiry which would keep a generation of legislative scholars busy and out of trouble.

I. Never the Twain Shall Meet

Even in a country where a fairly high percentage of a sample of the populace manages to miss almost any political question, it is a fair bet that most people know that our government is based on a separation of powers, modified somewhat by so-called checks and balances. Perhaps some of that group also know that this formula is supposed to protect the people from tyranny, and that our forefathers were confident it would. Their confidence was shared by most of the liberal philosophers of their time. But the Founding Fathers were, above all else, practical men; they were not so much

interested in a scientific separation of powers as they were in drawing on the lessons of experience to make a workable structure for
the future. What they did do in deference to that shibboleth of
separation which has had such an enormous influence on American political history was to provide in their Constitution that a
man who holds office in one branch cannot simultaneously serve
in another. At the same time, they softened the separation with
checks and balances, drawing again upon experience, and by the
admirable terseness of the document which they drew, they left
their equally pragmatic descendants largely free to distribute and
share powers as current exigencies seemed to require. The result
is an untidy but, on the whole, eminently successful system. Nevertheless, there have been and are tensions in the system produced
by contrary pulls of separation and commingling. Let us look first
at some of the effects of separation and later at the numerous
accommodations between legislature and executive which have
worked to dampen those effects.

SEPARATE SYSTEMS OF POWER

The process by which the English Parliament developed responsible
party government is too well known to need repeating. Why should
not the American system go the same way—to the extent the Constitution permits? A President elected by a majority of the people,
working through a majority of his own party in Congress, should
be able to enact a fair share of the program he has promised. Only
some structural changes—policy committees made up of committee
chairmen to adopt appropriate bills, party caucuses to pledge support to them—reinforced by a measure of public understanding
of the value of responsible parties, are needed, according to earnest
critics. Why have not such steps been taken? Why, in houses where
most partisans vote with a majority of their party most of the time,
do the blandishments of the President go unheeded, often at the
most critical times?

The fragmentation of party power followed naturally from the
need of Congress to establish some source of information separate
from the executive and some mechanism for independent consider-

ation of the merits of bills. In a parliamentary system the members can, at least in good logic, listen to the bureaucracy, because their own leaders are said to control the bureaucracy. But in the congressional system the bureaucrats are "they"; the men who more or less control them belong to the President. A committee was the answer: first an *ad hoc* committee, then a standing committee, then a standing committee with specialized jurisdiction. Such a committee perforce becomes a locus of power. So in time do its own subcommittees which, often over the strenuous exertions of the committee chairman, also carve out jurisdictions which they are quick to defend.

Even the dispersal of power in a committee system might not be irreparable if a party leadership could select the chairmen. But this is an exhausting procedure, often holding up appointments until most of the business is settled. The answer, as everyone knows, has been chairmanship selection by seniority, which often brings good and experienced men to power but which also, by definition, elevates those least answerable to a central party leadership. The President is not unlike a king forced to deal with feudal barons. He has certain advantages of identity with the national interest and superior visibility, as the king did, but he too must respect the rules of the game, which limit severely what he can command.

When these factors are reinforced by all the forces of localism inherent in federalism, accentuated by a long history on a vast continent with poor communication, the basic underpinnings of responsible party government are lacking.

Separate Institutional Influences on Behavior

The separation of personnel in the American system means a separation of *institutions*, and that separation has, in behavioral terms, profound influence on the day-to-day operations of American government. The Constitution, to repeat, says simply that the same man cannot hold office in both branches at the same time. A parliamentary system may actually separate powers very neatly; the minister may distinguish nicely between his executive and his legislative role. But he *can* have both roles at the same time, and so mediate between the legislature as an institution and the executive as an institution. Not so here; the institutions are clearly divided and so are the roles that go with each. What this means in behavioral terms is worth some exploration.

No dissertation on the term "institution" need be attempted. We mean simply a pattern of behavior of great stability and predictability, including the expectations people have that the pattern will be maintained. People know what behavior to expect in a church, a court of law, a college classroom. It is convenient but not essential to have an appropriate building and symbolic trappings; men have made and accepted a church in the hold of a ship at sea. What is necessary is that the participants behave according to expectations. Confusion comes when behavior appropriate to one institution is employed in another. This was the case in the televised controversy between Senator McCarthy and the Army, in which some judicial forms were bootlegged into a legislative hearing. On the other hand, appropriate behavior validates the collective actions people take.

If men brought up in our tradition were cast upon a desert island, they would know (without a political scientist among them) that policy should be adopted by a majority, that a project should have a leader, and that an accused man should be tried by his peers, however ignorant or biased they might be. It is accepted procedure, appropriate behavior, that legitimizes social action. The social function of a court, say, is not so much the administration of justice (who can say when it deals justly?) as it is the deciding of quarrels and the imposing of sanctions, even to the taking of life, in a way society accepts as legitimate.

Needless to say, men who are inducted into any social system in which they hope to be accepted try to learn the appropriate behavior. The literature on this process of socialization is extensive and need not be reviewed here. What is worth emphasis is that men who spend much or most of their adult lives in a social system as highly institutionalized as Congress and the bureaucracy, where careers are long and status and influence depend so much on tenure, are profoundly shaped in their attitudes by the institution itself. The institution is not the only or necessarily even the most important influence, of course, but its effect can be seen in some of the ineradicable suspicions and aversions which legislators and administrators develop toward each other, which persist even when they work productively and cooperatively together. The principal purpose of this essay will be to suggest some of the differences in the institutional fabric of legislature and executive, and the influence these differences have on the people who are associated with them.[1]

It should go without saying that the Court is a distinct institution, encrusted with the habits of centuries.[2] Like the Presidency and Congress, it is a political (as well as a legal) institution, sharing their power to make choices as to who shall get what. The Court—and especially the Supreme Court of the United States—legislates boldly and with remarkable political acumen, pushing to the testing point what Congress and the country will take. We leave it out of our discussion only because it is not part of the problem we have chosen to consider.

---

[1] A good picture of the life of a member of the House of Representatives may be found in Charles Clapp, *The Congressman: His Work as He Sees It* (Washington, D.C.: The Brookings Institution, 1963) and Clem Miller (ed. John W. Baker), *Member of the House: Letters of a Congressman* (New York: Charles Scribner's Sons, 1962). The life of the Senate is depicted in William S. White, *Citadel* (New York: Harper and Row, Publishers, Inc., 1956) and Donald R. Matthews, *U.S. Senators and Their World* (Chapel Hill: University of North Carolina Press, 1960). A pioneering investigation of the role perceptions of members of four state legislatures is that of John C. Wahlke, Heinz Eulau, William Buchanan, and LeRoy Ferguson, *The Legislative System: Explorations in Legislative Behavior* (New York: John Wiley and Sons, Inc., 1962). If my hypothesis that the legislature *as an institution* affects the behavior of its members is correct, the significance of the latter work for students of Congress is obvious.

[2] The influence of the court on its members has frustrated presidents throughout our history. For an interesting contemporary example of a dramatic conversion, see the account of the transformation of Mississippi's Supreme Court Justice Tom P. Brady from a race-baiting white supremacist to a champion of the U.S. Constitution in *Time,* October 22, 1965, pp. 94–96.

It is not quite accurate to say that we will contrast legislature and executive; what we really mean in the latter case is the bureaucracy. The political officers of the executive branch are a different breed than the bureaucrats. They form a kind of quasi-institution. They are not self-selected, as congressmen generally are, nor do they enjoy the tenure of either the bureaucracy or most members of Congress. They are creatures of the President, existing officially on sufferance. Their institutional life and influence on the system have largely escaped analysis and that is a pity.[3] The bureaucracy, on the other hand, is as old as human organization, and its habits, cries, and protective coloration have been subjected to intensive analysis. Moreover, it should be a safe wager that bureaucratic influence far outweighs that of the political executive officers, excepting possibly the President himself.

A good place to begin a study of any institution in which people make a living is with the conditions of employment. How are jobs got and kept? What influences salaries and promotions? These considerations probably influence the performance of professors, to take a ready example, more than the standard protestations of university presidents about the relative importance of good teaching.

The differences in the vocational aspects of the two branches of the national government are striking. The congressman is a politician whose first rule of life is to take care of himself. Characteristically, he is self-selected and self-promoted. It is he who decides that the public needs him in the first place and it is he who must persuade the public this is so at each election. Generally speaking, the national party cannot help him or hurt him very much. If the local party organization is strong, this simply means that the self-

[3] Richard E. Neustadt, in David B. Truman, ed., *The Congress and America's Future* (Englewood Cliffs, N.J.: Prentice-Hall, Inc., 1965), pp. 116–20, makes an interesting case for the common stakes of elective politicians. His viewpoint is primarily that of an acute observer of the executive branch. See also Dean E. Mann (with Jameson W. Doig), *The Assistant Secretaries: Problems and Processes of Appointment* (Washington, D.C.: The Brookings Institution, 1965).

selection process must employ other channels. His tenure likewise depends mostly upon his own efforts; he can be a statesman only so long as the people in his constituency are willing to let him be one.

The bureaucracy is another matter. The bureaucracy is peopled overwhelmingly by men and women who came into the service through a merit system examination, who rise in grade through largely non-competitive promotions, and who can look forward to retirement on a rather generous retirement plan. Everything in their professional lives underscores the slow but sure. They come to have faith in rules and procedures. The elements of risk and combat, of rewards and punishments that often are disproportionate and unfair—elements with which politicians live daily—are minimized.

It would seem reasonable to assume that self-selection assures generally that different kinds of men go into the separate branches. Certainly it is doubtful that either the politician or the bureaucrat could breathe easily in the environment of the other. Be that as it may, the distinct demands of each branch enforce differences.

A congressman may come from any vocation and he is required by his job to be a generalist. It is true that he specializes somewhat on his committee, and indeed may develop considerable expertise. Nevertheless, he is required to vote on a staggering variety of complicated bills, about most of which he will try to have at least a minimum understanding. The bureaucrat, on the other hand, is virtually required to be a specialist of some sort. Even if he is one of that handful of college graduates who come in as some kind of management intern, he soon finds his niche and concentrates on it if he is to move up the ladder. He is accustomed to operations in which a wide variety of experts can be brought to bear on a problem. As a matter of course he refers problems to the specialists whose skills are most appropriate to them.

The institutional fabrics into which these different kinds of men fit themselves are likewise distinctive. In Congress all members technically are peers, and at the time of the vote they are absolutely equal. The same weight of numbers which took the congressman to his house ultimately determines every issue on its floor. In the bureaucracy nothing is decided that way. The hierarchy of in-

fluence and responsibility is clearly understood; the distinctions between staff and line are appreciated; and status is reflected even in
the kinds of furniture permissible to an office and the order of
names on a route slip.

Furthermore, even the kinds of evidence which are acceptable
in these different kinds of institutions are sharply differentiated. A
congressional committee makes no attempt to get all the facts and
may joyfully accept what it knows not to be facts. It is interested
in hearsay, in opinion, in the shibboleths, however nonrational,
around which men rally and fight. This is not to discount the careful amassing of expert testimony which many committees do; the
point is simply that Congress is a representative assembly, a popularly elected body, and what may be studiously ignored in a courtroom may be exactly what a congressional committee most needs
to hear. The bureaucracy, on the other hand, is a matchless ma-
chine for assembling all kinds of facts, for taking into account all
kinds of expert advice. Congress itself is ultimately utterly dependent on the bureaucracy for most of the information upon which it
acts.

The process by which each branch makes policy is likewise its
own. Congress makes policy deliberately. The laying down of rules
of general applicability for the future is its avowed business. Gen-
erality indeed is forced upon it by the complexity of modern life.
Legislatures learned more than a century ago that they cannot
legislate in detail for very much of the varied life they seek to regulate. The bureaucracy is capable of making policy determinations
of breathtaking scope, but theoretically at least its task is to "fill in
the details" of general policy, and its characteristic mode is day-
by-day administration, employing standards, rules, and similar bureaucratic tools to fashion a general design.

What has been said here is familiar; any student could elaborate
it from his classroom notes. The recitation nevertheless has a
point: in this national government of separated institutions different kinds of men, operating in different kinds of institutional fabrics, proceed in different ways to perform much the same functions
for the political system. This has operational significance: the lead-

ers of pressure groups do not hesitate to seek from one branch what they fail to get from another but, unless they are incredibly naïve, they will adapt themselves carefully to the behavior appropriate to each. It also has significance for understanding the tensions and suspicions between branches which are endemic in the system. Perhaps most important, it suggests the crucial influence of the institution itself, with all its historic antecedents, on the behavior of the people who make their lives in it.

II. But of Course They Do Meet

Despite what has been said so far, the element of collaboration between Congress and executive is far more decisive in the operation of the American system than the fact of physical separation; law and the imperatives of politics require it to be. The modifications of separation affected by the checks and balances, incorporated in the Constitution more as accommodations to experience than as an exercise in theory, is in law quite substantial. There is no need to itemize the familiar constitutional assignments of power to make the point. In practice, the separation breaks down even more. It is trite to mention the familiar designation of the President as "chief legislator." He has accepted the role happily, sending a steady stream of messages and bills to Congress in the opening months of each session. Congress, on the other hand, appears to take seriously its obligation to supervise the administration of legislation. In the Legislative Reorganization Act of 1946, Congress assigned oversight responsibility along with legislative jurisdiction to its standing committees. Congress also has invented a score of devices for "overseeing administration" (or for "meddling," depending upon the point of view). Some of the most recent—and annoying to administrators—are the use of formal legal devices to give congressional committees the last word over certain kinds of administrative actions. Probably, much more important in the long run is the growing practice of the House of Representatives of passing one-year authorizations, requiring agencies to pass bills over again next year.

Needless to say, if legislative advice has not been heeded in that first year, unhappy accountings must be made in the second year. It may be, however, that the real significance of the one-year authorization is that the legislative committees in the House are jealous of the Appropriations Committee and do not wish to see it exercise the only check on the administration of programs during the several years of their authorized life.

The exercise of commingled powers is carried out by the two branches with a degree of pragmatism which reduces complaints of violations and overreachings to the level of political rhetoric. As Roland Young pointed out in his fine study of congressional politics in World War II, neither Congress nor the President has much to say about encroachments when the result achieved is good.[4] It is when a particular venture goes badly that the other side is open to the charge of constitutional poaching.

Even when all this is admitted, as it would readily be by sophisticated observers, there is not much in the literature which describes the extent to which the executive and legislature share the policy process at almost every turn. It is not easy to generalize from the rich and varied studies of particular aspects of the relationship which do exist. Subject to the test of systematic analysis, I suggest that Congress plays rather a more important part in legislation than its critics usually suggest, and that it would be easy to overstate what Congress does to supervise administration.

CONGRESS AS LEGISLATURE

Some critics have assigned Congress largely a passive role in legislation. It has been suggested that the President now initiates, Congress reacts.[5] This is superficially true. Even when the impetus comes from Congress, as it did in the legislative response to Sputnik, congressional leaders like to wait for the Administration bill

[4] Roland Young, *Congressional Politics in the Second World War* (New York: Harper and Row, Publishers, Inc., 1956).
[5] Samuel P. Huntington, "Congressional Responses to the Twentieth Century," in David B. Truman, ed., *op. cit.*, pp. 22–25.

to have something to work on. But what is easy to miss is the origin of many bills which in time pick up enough support to become "Administration bills." One or more members of Congress may have originated the idea and done all the spade work necessary to make it viable. One thinks of the lonely voice of George Norris in the 1920's calling for a Federal river project which became, in a different political climate, the Tennessee Valley Authority.[6] Other crusades have taken less time to succeed. Area redevelopment and water pollution control are projects which began in Congress. Examples are offered in the absence of systematic analysis. It is worth mention that the individual member may engineer a public policy. I remember watching a Canadian audience, including many members of its Parliament, listen enthralled to the account of Congressman Thomas Curtis, a minority member from Missouri, of his successful effort to enact a law suggested by a woman constituent.

Needless to say, the committees of Congress maintain a large measure of control over what goes into a bill and what happens to it, regardless of its origin. A striking case occurred in the early days of the second session of the 89th Congress. The Administration had proposed the conversion of loans to college students of money directly supplied (90 per cent of it) by the government to private bank loans guaranteed by the government. There was much opposition to the proposal, based largely on the fear that the new program could not be put in operation soon enough to meet the needs of students that year. The subcommittee of the House Education and Labor Committee which handles higher education, chaired by Congresswoman Edith Green of Oregon, met in executive session and voted unanimously to keep the National Defense Education Act loan program as it was (i.e., a direct loan program). The reason given by Mrs. Green was that the colleges needed to know what they could count on for the next school year. What is significant is the absolute confidence of the subcommittee, challenged by

[6] Henry C. Hart, "Legislative Abdication in Regional Development," *The Journal of Politics,* XIII (1951), 393–417.

no one, that the change could not be made without their approval. If that confidence were not justified, the colleges obviously could not base their plans on the subcommittee action.

It may be remarked that this was a negative action. Critics of Congress, particularly those of the liberal persuasion, have emphasized that Congress is obstructive, that it cannot act affirmatively.[7] As presidents have encountered obstacles to liberal programs, these critics have urged overhaul of structure and procedure to make Congress more responsible (i.e., more responsive to the President and the constituency that nominates and elects him). But in the first session of the 89th Congress, with a topheavy Democratic majority that included some seventy generally liberal freshmen, President Johnson got approval of a massive domestic legislative program that might normally have taken twenty years. The critics were not mollified. It was the work of a transient political genius, they said; soon Congress would go back to its normal nay-saying role. But such was not the case. In the second year of that Congress the President decided, under the pressure of war and threatened inflation, to hold the line on spending. The committees in both houses, legislative and appropriations alike, would have none of it; they set about expanding the programs of the year before and inventing new ones. This bit of legislative history may require a simple explanation: that elections do count and representation does work.

Emphasizing the congressional role in legislation is not an exercise in redundancy; it is given pertinence by the volume of literature arguing that Congress is impotent. It would be misleading, nevertheless, not to put Congress in the context of a system and suggest the roles of other participants. The notion of a legislative system that includes executive, courts, interest groups, press, local constituencies, and perhaps others, is useful but not precise enough. It might be more helpful to conceive of a set of "policy systems," in which all parties involved in a particular category of issues share

[7] For a selection of the writings critical of Congress, see my "Democratic Party Leadership in the Senate," *American Political Science Review,* LV (June 1961), 333–44.

regularly in the making, alteration, and execution of policy. This would recognize the specialization necessary to effective political action. A particular policy is made by the people in the agencies, public and private, who are interested in and know about that policy area. There is an almost continuous interchange among committee members, their staffs, the executive (that is, agency personnel, White House staff, and private persons appointed to "task forces," and the like) and representatives of private associations at almost every stage of the process, from the first glimmer of an idea to compromises in conference and to administration of the act.[8] Careful research would be necessary to establish the extent to which these generalizations are true and where the breakdowns occur, but it is a fair guess that members of the appropriate committees are seldom if ever taken by surprise by executive initiative in legislation. Indeed, much initiation is simply the reasonable next step in the view of those within a given policy system and it is so recognized on all sides, even though there is opposition to it.

CONGRESS AS OVERSEER

The relationship of Congress to the administrative performance of the bureaucracy is equally important and invites careful study.[9] Students of representative assemblies at least since the time of John Stuart Mill have said that control of the government—the oversight function—is probably the most important task the legislature performs. It is easy to get the impression that the bureaucracy lives under the heavy frown of congressional supervision all the time. Certainly it is not pleasant to be interrogated by a congressional committee, nor to find oneself in the headlines which are congenial

[8] For an example of this, see Stephen K. Bailey's classic case study, *Congress Makes a Law* (New York: Columbia University Press, 1950). Ernest S. Griffith refers to this coalescence of interests as a "whirlpool" in his *Congress: Its Contemporary Role,* 3rd ed. (New York: New York University Press, 1961).

[9] For a careful analysis of the process, see Joseph P. Harris, *Congressional Control of Administration* (Washington, D.C.: The Brookings Institution, 1964).

to the politician but not to the civil servant. But for the most part it is the politicians in the agencies, the expendable men, who face the committees in open hearings. Congressmen complain that they reach understandings with the political people which are not kept by the agency's operating personnel, who are largely beyond the reach of Congress. Without careful comparative studies designed to explore the range of patterns of relations which exist, it is hazardous to suggest generalizations. But perhaps it is not out of order to make some tentative comments based on observation.

The first would be the prediction that appropriate studies will show that not much "oversight" of administration, in a systematic and continuous enough manner to make it mean very much, is practiced. The appropriations committees probably do more than the legislative committees (which, not surprisingly, are more interested in legislation), and the House Appropriations Committee does more than the Senate committee (because it is bigger, hears the agencies first, and permits its members no other committee assignments). Most legislative oversight occurs when hearings on new bills or authorizations occur. Closer scrutiny is likely to result from the personal interest of a chairman or ranking member, the sudden interest of the public in a program or a member's hunch that interest can be aroused, or the relationship (amounting virtually to institutional incest in a separation-of-powers system) which arises when a chairman fills the agency's top jobs with his own former staff members. The individual member's interest in administration is likely to be spurred by a constituent's protest, which subsides when the matter is taken care of.

III. What Should Be Done

If the argument in the beginning of this essay—that there are similarities among particular political institutions in roughly comparable systems and that these institutional influences significantly affect behavior—has merit, then research on the legislature might profitably attempt to be comparative.

Comparative studies of legislative-administrative relations in the English parliamentary and the American presidential-congressional systems, as an example, might be worth doing. The legislature and bureaucracy in both countries stem from the same root, the feudal Great Council which advised the king. Some of its members were barons who belonged to the Curia Regis, a part of his permanent court which developed into the professional bureaucracy. The other members of the Great Council were barons invited, usually three times a year, to consult with the king and consent to taxes. They were joined in time by representatives of the communities. From these occasional meetings the bicameral legislature evolved, while the professional bureaucracy is an outgrowth of the Curia Regis itself. Thus it is that our practices and procedures (and this is true of our courts as well) bear everywhere the marks of English experience. These are worth tracing and explaining.

But our histories have diverged and there are differences. Leaving aside the tendency of some Americans to idealize the British system, what price have we paid in friction and inefficiency for an arrangement which forces the legislature and bureaucracy to negotiate without the legislator-minister as intermediary? Is that lack so decisive as some other factors that accompany it? Say, that the Member of Parliament generally is powerless to do much and the Member of Congress is not? Or that the Member of Parliament may hope for genuine power only in the executive (and so shapes his efforts that way) while a ranking Member of Congress almost surely would sacrifice power if he were to join the executive? To what extent, on the other hand, has institutional separation been bridged in the American system by the shared interest and expertise of committee and agency people, and by their mutual dependence? These questions lead not to statements of abstractly ideal systems but to an attempt to weigh the costs and gains of alternative arrangements.

What is most difficult, obviously, is to sort and assess the relative weights of influences that bear on a man in public life. The argument of this essay is that the institutional influence is a powerful one, that it shapes attitudes and values and produces a shared way of life—so much so that a seasoned member of almost any legislature in the Western world almost surely would be more at home on the floor of either house of the American Congress than most American bureaucrats would be. If this is so, it suggests that the influence of an institution in all its historic dimensions may be stronger than those which are products of a peculiar national experience. The hypothesis should be worth exploring.

The idea of studying the legislature—or any other political institution—in a comparative way is attractive. If political systems may profitably be compared, why not political institutions? It may be that legislatures appear in a system at a certain stage of development, that they perform similar political functions whatever the system, that they affect the behavior of their members in ways that are enough alike to be significant.

Needless to say, there is much of crucial importance to be done on Congress without regard to other systems or to other institutions within the American system.[10] Research on Congress with a behavioral bent has come a long way, it seems to me, in the last ten or twelve years. Our discipline has produced a generation of scholars sensitive to the influence on the behavior of congressmen of the various roles they assume in the related subsystems of Congress, and to the influence on Congress of the external system with which it interacts. We have sliced into our problem enough ways to give us a notion of what is there and some confidence that we know how to proceed. What we still lack, even with the extensive descriptive and prescriptive work of several generations of predecessors, is any very clear idea, to put it simply, of how Congress works—how its principal parts do their jobs and how they are related to each other.

---

[10] Most of the remaining material is taken from a working paper prepared by the author for a conference of congressional scholars who met at Airlie House, Warrenton, Virginia, on May 20, 1964, to launch the American Political Science Association's Study of Congress. The Study of Congress is financed by the Carnegie Corporation and directed by the author and Robert L. Peabody. Most of the topics upon which scholars of the Study of Congress are working were taken generally from these suggestions.

Empirical research can and should provide us with analytical descriptions of Congress, its subsystems, and its relations with its environment; these should (1) fill in the research gaps, suggesting models and relevant variables for future research; and (2) provide some basis for stating the functions Congress performs for the political system, evaluating the performance, and pointing out alternative structural arrangements and modes of action which seem realistically to be open to Congress. Until we have reasonably adequate models, can identify significant variables, and can know what a deceptively simple action like a recorded vote probably means, the machines stand ready to give us more help than we can use. Until we have some idea about what needs of the system are served by Congress and how it serves them, the laundry-ticket lists of congressional reforms are no more than statements of personal preferences.

Research on Congress might be categorized many ways. The categories which will be suggested here are no better than some others that might be chosen, but they should help to organize discussion. Two categories that are obvious enough are the internal system, with its norms and roles, and the relations of this system with the external system, its environment. A third category might be that of policy, or process; the budget or economic policy or foreign policy or defense, might be considered, with the approach not separating internal and external systems, but combining them as the legislative system for that kind of policy. A fourth category might deal with purely facilitative concerns. What kinds of changes would help Congress get on with its job, whatever that job is conceived to be? Improvements in personnel recruitment, pay for congressmen, vacations, scheduling, and other items affecting the congressman's life might readily fall into a single category, perhaps even into a single study.

THE INTERNAL SYSTEM

The study of the power structure of each house—and they probably should be studied separately—might begin with the elected leaders.[11] We should not be satisfied with a description of the way the present incumbents operate; this would be little more than good journalism, at best. What is the range of behaviors open to the incumbent of a leadership position? What rewards and punishments were available to Mr. Rayburn in the time of his maximum prestige? What does an intangible like "prestige" mean and how can it be translated into power? What happened in the years of Mr. Rayburn's waning personal powers? How does the House work, when the Speaker is ineffective? A close study of the division of labor among the elected leadership on both sides of the aisle, preferably with some attention to history to gain some sense of alternative possibilities, might require the collaboration of several people.

The Senate clearly is a separate study. The floor leadership seems to vary even more widely with incumbent and circumstance than the Speakership; it has fewer institutional props to support it. One crucial variable certainly is the leader's own perception of his role. Another is the occupant of the White House, whether he is of the same party as the Senate majority, and if so, what he expects of the leader and what their relations are. How can the formal party organs, such as the policy committees and the conferences, be used? Recent history suggests a cynical answer, but less recent history does not; Wilson's leader relied heavily on the conference in one of the most productive legislative periods in our history and there are senators now who argue the conference need not be useless.

In each house, the relations of the elected leaders with the committee chairmen should be explored. How does a "strong" elected leader approach his chairmen? Does he attempt to establish priorities among bills? Influence their content? Or does he just take the committee product and try to move it on the floor? These questions are doubly complicated in the House by the power of the Rules Committee. Recent history suggests at least superficially that the Speaker's principal tool is a showdown or threat of it, a weapon as

---

[11] See David B. Truman, *The Congressional Party* (New York: John Wiley and Sons, Inc., 1959); Ralph K. Huitt, "Democratic Party Leadership in the Senate," *op. cit.*; Charles O. Jones, *Party and Policy-making* (New Brunswick, N.J.: Rutgers University Press, 1964).

likely to blow up as it is to shoot. But what about periods when Speaker and committee chairmen worked in close accord? What then was their relation with strong committee chairmen?

Perhaps no study could be more rewarding than a systematic comparative analysis of committees. Some useful and suggestive work already has been done. How do the norms of other committees differ from those found by Professor Richard Fenno to prevail in the House Appropriations Committee?[12] Are the norm systems different and more permissive in less prestigious committees? How are members recruited to committees? What does the freshman member know about this fateful decision about his career? What kind of socialization does he go through?

The chairmen should be the targets of close analysis. This means, among other things, scrutiny of the operation of seniority. It is easy to attack or defend seniority; what does not commend itself to scholarship apparently is the empirical question of its effects. How many committee majorities actually are frustrated by the tyranny of their seniority chairmen? How is this putative authoritarianism accomplished? Can committee majorities break out? What rules do they need—or are the rules already on the books? What happens when a new chairman faces 180 degrees away from his predecessor (say, Langer succeeds McCarran, Eastland follows Kilgore, on Senate Judiciary)? How does a committee deal with a senile chairman? Are there institutional devices for going around him and how well do they work? Answers to questions like these can take a lot of the fun out of the debate over seniority.

Relations among committees also are important. We think especially of the experience of legislative committees which see their floor successes at the authorization stage put in hazard by the appropriations committees. And the relations of the spending with the taxing committees. What problems come from the inescapable overlapping of committee jurisdictions? How do like committees in the two houses get along? Why do the two spending committees

---

[12] "The House Appropriations Committee as a Political System: The Problem of Integration," *American Political Science Review*, LVI (June 1962), 310–24.

often fight when the taxing committees collaborate easily and well? Who wins in conference? Does it vary from committee to committee? Does the seniority system at the conference stage really deliver control of the ultimate product to the oligarchies of the houses?

The norm system in the Senate has been studied to some effect, but the same cannot be said for the House.[13] Both chambers are worth more attention. What is the range of permissible behavior in each? Systematic analyses of the "outsider," who helps to define the norms by pressing at their boundaries, might be useful. What are the sanctions in these institutionalized groups which have almost no control over the selection of their members? Who is the "outsider"? Is he a personality type? Are there significant correlations with state or district, with socio-psychological origins? In what ways may he be said to be "effective"? In what ways may he be functional, in what ways dysfunctional, for the system?

The chamber floor as terrain for legislative combat might also be a focus of study. What is the relationship between the formal and the informal rules? What advantages, if any, does the skilled parliamentarian enjoy? What difference would a change in rules make? What are the strategies which might be employed by the men who lead floor fights? The literature recounts occasional coups by which advantage has been gained through knowledge and use of the rules. What is not clear is whether legislators divide labor as lawyers do, with a counterpart on the floor of the skilled advocate who takes the prepared case to the courtroom, or whether there is enough to parliamentary advocacy to justify specialization.

Another actor who occupies an ambiguous place in the power structure is the professional staff man,[14] an ambiguous figure because his influence has been both underrated and overrated. Surely he is more than a facilitator, more than extra hands to relieve the

---

[13] Matthews, *op. cit.*, Ch. 5; Huitt, "The Morse Committee Assignment Controversy: A Study in Senate Norms," *American Political Science Review*, XLI (June 1957), 313–29, and "The Outsider in the Senate," *ibid.*, LV (September 1961), 566–75.

[14] See Kenneth Kofmehl, *Professional Staffs of Congress* (West Lafayette, Indiana: Purdue University Press, 1962).

legislator of errand-running, more than a trained research mind to end legislative dependence on bureaucrat and lobbyist. Surely he is less than the real power behind the throne, as the frustrated lobbyist, and even the staff man himself, sometimes think he is. What is he like, this bright and ambitious man who submerges his own career aspirations in those of another? What does he want, what does he think he can get? How does *he* perceive his role, its satisfactions and limitations? Some remarkable men have served members of Congress; some have gone on to serve two presidents who have come out of the legislature. There is a great study to be made of the professional staff man and his relations with his principal by the legislative scholar who can enter upon it with his preconceptions firmly under control.

RELATIONS WITH THE EXTERNAL SYSTEM

The importance of the web of relationships existing between Congress and the President, bureaucracy, parties, interest groups, press, and constituencies is so patent that almost any well designed study of any of these relationships could have significance. Let me suggest only two or three.

One need which must be met before the computers really can serves us is the construction of more sophisticated models of systems of outside influence which press upon a member of Congress. The party is an example.[15] Many roll call studies have made use of "party votes," so designated because a stated majority of one party opposed a similar majority of the other. Indices of cohesion and other measures are built from them and statements are made about the influence of party on members or on this or that bloc. The curious thing is that our model of the party in the basic texts is much more sophisticated than that. A reasonably competent student in the freshman course can write that the major party "is a federation of state and local parties." Why is not this model carried over into research on Congress? Suppose that two members bearing the same

---

[15] An excellent bibliography on the subject has been compiled by Charles O. Jones and Randall B. Ripley, *The Role of Political Parties in Congress* (Tucson, Arizona: University of Arizona Press, 1966).

party designation split their votes on a roll call. Might it not be that one is voting with the national committee party, the other casting an opposing vote *with* a state or local party which bears the same name—in a word, *both* are casting party votes?

A similarly simplistic view of *the* constituency often is employed.[16] A conception of the constituency as all the people of voting age living in the district or state is bound to lead to remarkable results. Everyone knows that the constituency so conceived will have opinions on very few issues indeed. Nevertheless, the member talks about his constituency; he says he follows its wishes sometimes or all the time, and it is not safe to assume without proof that this is double-talk or that he is a dunce. On the contrary; his perhaps tacit concept of constituency is more complicated: he responds to *different* constituencies on different issues. He may try to paint an image of himself in the broadest strokes as an "economizer," say, for the vast number of voters who will try to remember *something* about him when they go to the polls, while at the same time he works to amend one line of a bill to please a half-dozen labor leaders who can make or break him by the kind of voter-registration effort they put on. These are "constituencies"— the people of varying degrees of influence, knowledge, and intensity of feeling who are aware of and respond to particular issues. The students of public opinion long ago learned that if they defined "public" as all the people living in a society there usually would be no public opinion. Because this was a nonsense result they defined the term in a variety of ways that would support analysis. That is what we must do with the concept "constituency."

Inasmuch as "party" and "constituency" in this sense are systems of influence, why not go for help with our models to the per-

[16] For sophisticated analyses of congressional relations with constituencies employing survey research techniques and systematic interviews, see Warren E. Miller and Donald E. Stokes, "Constituency Influence in Congress," *American Political Science Review,* LVII (March 1963), 45–56; and Charles C. Cnudde and Donald J. McCrone, "The Linkage Between Constituency Attitudes and Congressional Voting Behavior: A Causal Model," *ibid.,* LX (March 1966), 66–72.

sons presumably influenced, the members of Congress themselves? How do *they* perceive party and constituency? The same kinds of questions might be asked about interest groups, bureaucracy, or any other putative system of influence.

One further need may be suggested. In the systematic comparative study of committees close attention should be paid to the patterns of relations between committees and the bureaucratic agencies they supervise. An unassailable truism of legislative literature makes "legislative oversight" a basic congressional task. But what goes on under the label "oversight"? Consider some of the conventional tools. Appropriations: do the subcommittees really get to the heart of the matter? Investigation: is anything really changed after the dust settles? Confirmation: what difference does it really make in agency operations *who* the top man is? Detailed legislation: but isn't it the lesson of the last century that Congress must delegate to administrators the burden of legislating in detail? Studies of the oversight exercised by particular committees make clear that some of them exercise no supervision over the agencies assigned them and have no desire to do it; others have a variety of relationships, some of which would be hard to call oversight. What determines the character of the committee's concern about administrative performance? Some of the hypothetical variables are the personality of the chairman and his perception of his role, the character of the agency and its program, the degree of constituency involvement in the program, the character and quality of the committee's professional staff. Careful and realistic additions to the literature on oversight will find an eager audience among the bureaucrats themselves.

POLICY-MAKING PROCESS

It is not easy for a feudal system to make national policy. Whatever the advantages of dispersed centers of power (and I believe they are many), the capacity to make and carry out a plan is not among them. It is common for Congress to have inflationary and deflationary programs underway at the same time, to take away with one hand what it gives with the other. Some of our studies might profitably abandon the single house as a subsystem and look at the way one kind of policy is made across the board.[17] What is the budget process? This might be broken into spending and taxing (as Congress does it). How is foreign policy, or defense policy, fashioned? If Congress wanted to make a real effort to effect co-ordination in the making of some kind of national policy, what devices might be employed that have been proved by congressional experience to be useful for that purpose? If stronger party leadership generally were desired, what organizational arrangements might be strengthened, what inhibited? What would be gained and what would be the price?

These last questions, we might say finally, should be part of every study. Congress changes, as all living things must change; it changes slowly, adaptively, as institutions change. But structural arrangements are not neutral; they will be used by those who can get control of them for whatever purposes the controllers have in mind. Changes, therefore, may have unforeseen consequences. What changes seem possible of accomplishment, given Congress's history and present structure? Who seems likely to benefit, who will pay? These are questions our discipline has taught us to ask.

---

[17] For representative studies, see Holbert N. Carroll, *The House of Representatives and Foreign Affairs* (Pittsburgh: University of Pittsburgh Press, 1958); Aaron Wildavsky, *The Politics of the Budgetary Process* (Boston: Little, Brown and Co., 1964).

Power in Congress

Clem Miller

The essay that follows is a brilliant description of the workings of Congress as seen by one of its own members. Writing between 1959 and 1961, the late congressman from California sought to inform, through a series of newsletters, certain of his constituents about the activities of Congress. The result is one of the most candid and informative descriptions of Congress at work that has yet been written.

It is clear from Congressman Miller's account that there is present in the Congress the kind of institutional compulsion to appropriate behavior about which Mr. Huitt wrote in the previous selection. The path to power in the House of Representatives is different from what it would be in another institution of government, and it is patent that the reason for this lies in large part with the institutional expectations and conventions of the House. Mr. Justice Jackson of the Supreme Court once observed that the Court influences the justices more than the justices influence the Court. Clearly, much the same thing is true of Congress, and Congressman Miller helps us to understand how this is so.

SOURCE: Clem Miller, *Member of the House: Letters of a Congressman,* ed. John Baker (New York: Scribner's, 1962), ch. 3, pp. 95–115. Copyright © 1962 by Charles Scribner's Sons and reprinted with their permission.

"Power" is an ambiguous term, but as Miller uses it here it means the ability to get something done or to prevent something from being done. A member of Congress must learn how power is wielded in Congress; it is not an abstract exercise but rather one of utter concreteness. Congress offers a unique arena in which the points of decision making are dispersed and are subject to influence only if its uniqueness is appreciated. A large part of that uniqueness consists of the expectations of one's colleagues, which are in turn shaped by the institutionalized behavior of the membership. Some members of Congress learn this lesson early; some never learn it at all. The result is that power, and powerlessness, in Congress is in part a function of reputation, and reputations are shaped by the nature of Congress and the ability, or inability, of members to adapt themselves to that nature.

It is very much worth noting that the path to power and the path to publicity are in a genuine sense antithetical. The result is a common phenomenon in American political life: Some of the most notoriously ineffectual Congressmen are widely known to consumers of newspapers, radio, and television, while some of the most powerful members of Congress are scarcely known to the general public. Some choose the path of publicity consciously, but this very likely occurs, particularly among members of the Senate, because they are seeking the White House rather than congressional power.

The arts that accompany the ability to influence mass public opinion are not the arts required to influence colleagues in a legislative body. President Kennedy's career in Congress was not notable, but he was one of the most successful Presidents in employing the techniques of mass persuasion. President Johnson was one of the most influential Senators in the history of Congress, but, after his accession to the White House, he was faced with a crisis of public confidence that ultimately forced his retirement from office.

Congress, writes Mr. Miller, "is a collection of committees that come together in a Chamber periodically to approve one another's actions." This is not a textbook definition; it is rather the result of experience. But power in Congress can be exercised only by those who profit from experience. And the student of government who wishes to understand the apparently mysterious process by which things are done, or prevented from being done, in Congress can learn from the vicarious experience afforded by the selection that follows.

The word "power" has been defined in many ways. It may refer to the strength which a nation has in influencing or controlling other nations. If one speaks of individual power, he may mean the ability to control or to influence others either by physical force, craft, or leadership. In the sense that the term power is used with reference to Congress, the definition "ability to do or act; capability of doing or effecting something" applies. A person who has power in Congress is someone who can get things done or who can keep things from being done if he so desires. It is obvious that no person has complete power. Congress is not a rubber stamp for an individual or even a small group of individuals. But there are powerful congressmen, and there are congressmen who are almost totally ineffective. There are always leaders, men of power, natural leaders in any group. Most of the Members of Congress are or have been leaders; if this were not so they never would have been elected. Why then do some congressmen have power and others seem to get nowhere despite their heroic efforts?

Power does not come necessarily from party regularity. Many powerful people constantly disagree with other powerful people of the same party. Wilson said, "Power is nowhere concentrated; it is rather deliberately and of set policy scattered amongst many small chiefs." This is a way of defining power in terms of the mechanics of organization. The two loose confederations in the House which we call political parties organize the House. The leader of the majority party becomes the Speaker. Committee assignments are made on the basis of seniority in the House. The freshmen start out on an equal footing, with some getting more desirable assignments than others. Rankings within a committee are based on seniority in that particular committee, and the chairman and a majority of the members are from the majority party in the House. Seniority is the key to assignment and, as such, is the key to tremendous power.

Power is personal as well as hierarchical. It springs from . . . rules and precedents . . . . It may come to some outside the upper levels of the hierarchy. It never comes to a freshman!

The following letters give a glimpse of how power functions in the House—how things are done, how changes are effected.

Dear Friend:

Last week in the House of Representatives a southern freshman addressed the Members in his maiden remarks. In part, this is what he said: ". . . there is definite evidence that subversive activities are at the base or at the root of our school problems in the South."

The story of how this gentleman came to attain his seat in the face of grave and troublesome election irregularities may be set forth as a compound of precedent, procedure, maneuver, and power. Many of us were disarmed at the start by an agreement that he should stand aside while everyone else was sworn in. (He was then sworn in at a separate ceremony pending investigation of his status.) We were further beguiled by the rumor which was spread through the halls that he would be seated, but not as a Democrat. The fact is that he will take his seat after exhaustive hearings, and he now is listed in the directories as a Democrat.

How does this happen? Why doesn't the substantial majority which would oppose seating this man register protests? First, there is the hard certainty that he would be overwhelmingly reelected if we should refuse to seat him. The futility of such a gesture is a depressant action. Second, there is precedent, that most powerful of House levers. And precedents are against us in this case. We have seated all kinds of men in the past—men guilty of fraud, felony, and every kind of irregularity. These factors weighed heavily in this case.

And finally there are the procedures of the House which work for the man. One must comprehend that all House action springs from one committee or another. It is by means of the committee process that the 435 Members of the House are held to some semblance of order, and that the work of Congress is organized and put through. This monolithic, glacial action is refined to an even finer tolerance by our committee chairman. In this particular case, we felt an issue should be made of party affiliation. The question is how party responsibility can be built if office holders drift in and out of their party at will. And on this point, we were told that the man's committee appointment would be taken out of the Republican committee quota and that he would be seated as an Independent. Then, when nothing could be done about it, the Committee on Committees reported out the full list of committee assignments. The new man was at the very bottom, but carried as a Democrat. When the matter came to the Floor, as a committee matter, backed up by the tremendous prestige of its chairman, one would have had to vote against himself in order to vote against the report. It came before Congress in its entirety. The opposition had been neatly fragmented into seventy-eight pieces. The matter was closed.

It is probably difficult for those of you at home to understand how this apparently placid maneuver could take place. It is not difficult to see from here. As newcomers, without organization, without the sense of trust and interdependence that comes from long association, we lack any locus of power. The interior lines of communication and strength are contained in the hands of those who have been here for many years. The organization and procedures of the House make it well-nigh impossible to speak out as an individual. And it is unwise to speak out as a group unless (a) you have the votes to win, or (b) you have a really grand canvas upon which to spread a public protest. The progressive leaders felt that this case did not present the scope for such a protest. A big price must be paid for defeat. When you pay that price, the resulting public achievement must be worth it.

But the gentleman in question has put the South on the spot as well as the nation, and a lot of southern congressmen are privately unhappy. Every district has an extremist who can outshout any incumbent. One congressman confided that such a person in his district could beat him. He said, "I believe in law and order. When it comes to defying the law, I've got to step aside. I've got to fight for our laws." This congressman would be an easy mark for a demagogue.

Very sincerely,
Clem Miller

Dear Friend:

I have been trying to describe and delineate the troubles and problems of political leadership as well as those of party responsibility in the House. There are similar problems in the Senate. Here, in my mind, is an excellent insight which I hope you will find interesting. It was in the February 5th "Congressional Report" of the National Committee for an Effective Congress:[1]

On January 12, 1960, meeting in closed session, the Democratic members of the Senate voted 51–12 to defeat a motion by Albert Gore of Tennessee, and 51–11 to pass a motion by Mike Mansfield of Montana.

These results were conveyed immediately to fifty-odd newspaper and broadcasting people camped in the corridor outside, and a few minutes later were trumpeted to the nation as another stunning defeat for the "liberals."

The general public was given an impression—doubly false, but strangely satisfying to the die-hards on both sides—that the "liberals" have less than a third of the strength they normally muster on substantive issues, and that Johnson is a kind of Congressional Carmine de Sapio riding roughshod over all opposition.

So ended what the *Washington Post* casually dismissed as the liberals' "annual uprising" against the leadership. What really happened, and how significant was it? . . . When William Proxmire called last year for "regular caucuses (on) our legislative program," he was seek-

[1] This article originally appeared in the *St. Louis Post-Dispatch* and is reprinted here with their permission.

ing to reverse a leadership situation that had developed without design over half a century. Fifty years ago, the Senate Democratic caucus, or conference, was a powerful instrument. A vote of two-thirds of its members was binding upon each individual Senator and determined his vote on the floor. This system broke down after World War I, following the passage of the 17th amendment, which provided for direct election of Senators. As long as Senators had been elected by state legislatures, they could afford to make the deals implicit in accepting the discipline of the caucus; once they had to justify themselves to the people, they could no longer accept that discipline. The system was almost completely eroded during the Roosevelt and Truman administrations, when legislative recommendations flowed from the White House and the task of the Democratic leadership was merely to see that they were processed as smoothly as possible.

Recently, virtually the only function of the Senate Democratic conference has been to elect the party's floor leader; and under Lyndon Johnson, conference meetings had been limited to one each year.

That this lack of conference activity could have lasted six years for a party without a President and as variously represented as the Democrats are in the Senate, is a tribute to Johnson's skill as a leader—to the perceptiveness with which he determined the consensus and the fidelity with which he represented it. . . .

There has always been a tendency among some to blame Johnson for what were, in fact, errors of the consensus. But now the situation has changed substantially. Now, even many of Johnson's more tolerant colleagues complain that he no longer represents the consensus; and that frequently he deliberately ignores it.

Several factors have helped to produce this change:

1. The balance of power within the Democratic Party in the Senate has shifted greatly as a result of the election in 1958 of large numbers of new Democrats from northern and western states. It is no longer so easy to play the two extremes against each other and come up on dead center.

2. The size of the Democratic majority tends to weaken discipline. The threat of a defection is not so frightening when it does not raise the possibility of Republicans taking over.

3. Scenting a possibility of winning the presidency for the first time in eight years, the northern and western members are less

inclined to be patient with a "stand pat" policy of bipartisan cooperation with the administration. . . .

Against this background, the real result of the meetings of the Democratic conference early this month was quite different from what was reported to the public.

The principle objective of the liberals was to secure additional meetings of the conference for discussion of substantive legislative issues. Senator Clark (Pa.) had prepared a resolution providing for such meetings to be held at the request of fifteen Senators, and it was expected that a fight would develop around this motion. However, as soon as the issue was raised at the meeting on January 7, Johnson said that he had "promised" in 1953 that a meeting would be called whenever requested by any individual Senator, and that the promise was still good.

This commitment was so sweeping that it aroused a degree of concern among some members as to the possibility that meetings might be called too lightly, and at the instance of colleagues seeking only personal publicity rather than serious attention to an issue. However, after some discussion, a consensus was reached as to calling meetings of the conference whenever one was seriously desired, and it was accepted without a vote that such a decision had been made and will be implemented. . . .

Only after this very substantial victory did there begin the maneuvers which got the play in the press and gave the appearance of a disastrous liberal defeat.

As described by *Senator A* (who voted *with Johnson*), Johnson took exception to some of the remarks that had been made during the discussion on conference meetings. He felt they reflected on his leadership, and made the "bad mistake" of getting angry. He called attention to the honored membership of the Policy Committee and implied that any criticism of him must also be taken as criticism of them. The Policy Committee does not, in fact, set policy. It merely determines the timing of the legislative schedule—and no one has had any complaint against it. But Johnson's anger so aroused some of the liberals that they immediately vowed to "do something" about the Policy Committee.

Another meeting was held on January 12, and the Gore resolution was not introduced until then. This resolution called for the enlargement of the Policy Committee, for its members to be elected by the conference rather than appointed by Johnson, and for the Committee to attempt to work out legislative policy lines for the Senate Democrats.

According to *Senator B* (who voted *against Johnson*), the issue posed by the Policy Committee resolution introduced by Senator Gore was not advantageously framed and little or no effort was made to enlist supporters for it. Both these facts contributed to, if they did not dictate, its defeat by a vote of 51–12. "It injected an entirely new issue which even we who voted with Gore had not thought through," the Senator said.

After more than two hours of discussion of the Gore resolution, and after it was voted down, Carroll (Colo.) rose to suggest that some thought be given to the possibility of electing members of the Steering Committee in the future. (This group makes the committee assignments which are the basis of senatorial careers. Its members presently are appointed by the leader.) Although Carroll had not made a motion, and merely suggested that thought be given to the idea, Johnson sensed an opportunity for another victory. Mansfield (Montana), the party whip, moved for a vote against changing the procedure for selection of Steering Committee members—and this carried by 51–11. Senator B thought this vote "involved a clear matter of principle, and many more of our friends should have been with us."

Senator C (who voted *with Johnson*) claims that no one seriously wanted the reforms which were rejected in these two votes. "The motions were made just to embarrass Johnson's presidential hopes," he said. "I voted against them for two reasons. First, however I may disagree with him sometimes, I think he has been a good enough leader not to deserve that kind of treatment from us. Second, we have other presidential candidates here, and we're not going to accomplish anything during this session if we all start playing this way."

Senator D (who voted *against Johnson*) said that the issue was whether the Democrats could begin to have a party position and project a party image. Having the Policy Committee try to chart party policy in the Senate might not work out, he said, "but we should at least experiment with it." Finding a successful formula by which Policy Committee drafts of positions would be amended or ratified by the conference at the beginning of each session "would enable the public to know whenever any Democrat votes like a Republican. There's too much of that going undetected now."

Senator E (who voted *with Johnson*) said even his liberal colleagues are too concerned with protecting the interest groups in their own states to be bound by either the Policy Committee or the conference. "I'd vote for it if they were willing to be bound," he declared, "but when Frear (Del.) pointed to each of them and asked if they would be bound they each said 'no.' What sense does that make? Also, I see no point in the meetings. We all know what the others think. The fellows who do all the talking on the floor (of the Senate) are the same ones who would do the talking at meetings. I'm too busy as things are to listen to any more. What would make some sense would be a liberal conference. The liberals in the House have a smart, well-organized and effective operation going (the Democratic Study Group, headed by Lee Metcalf of Montana). If the fellows on the same side here would try to work together, I'd be for that. But there are too many prima donnas here."

A final word was added by a *top Senate staff member* whose feelings toward the Leadership are such that he probably would have voted with the liberals had he been a Senator, but who would have had no confidence in that vote. "An elected Policy Committee would probably be worse than what Johnson has appointed," he said. "Under the seniority system, the senior members exert such influence over the votes of the junior members that they would effectively control the selection of the Policy Committee," he pointed out. "All Senators are equal, but some Senators are more equal than others, and Lyndon Johnson is the most equal. Fortunately," he concluded, "Johnson hasn't done badly by the liberals in making their own committee appointments, and in selecting the members of the Policy and Steering Committees."

The real and for the most part unreported significance of all this is revealed in the fact that a meeting of the Democratic conference was held the following week to discuss the education bill—the first meeting on a substantive issue since 1952. About half of the Democratic Senators attended and there was a spirited and genial discussion of the pending bill for federal aid for school construction. Senator Clark made a strong statement on behalf of his amendment for federal aid for teachers' salaries, and picked up sufficient support to introduce the amendment with twenty-two sponsors.

Although the leadership was present at this meeting, it was significant that most of the opponents of the bill did not attend. As a result, no differences of opinion were threshed out and no attempt was made to record a consensus. However, the meeting revealed, to those most interested in the bill, the extent of the support they could count on, and it provided an opportunity for discussion they might not otherwise have had. In this respect, it was worthwhile. Since additional meetings are expected to be held on other issues, a further evaluation of the significance of the "uprising" must await their results.

Very sincerely,
Clem Miller

Dear Friend:

Today I wish to return to the individual and his relation to power. An analogy with medieval warfare is suggested here. The congressman may seek to take the castle by scaling the walls in open combat or by a sapping operation under the moat. Scaling the walls means making many Floor speeches, getting in on every debate from railroad pensions to the color of oranges, putting on the hair shirt for the public and the press, etc. The structure of Congress consigns this course to almost certain failure. The very qualities of public show, of defiance, of bravery, are looked at askance. The congressman who speaks constantly, even if cogently, cannot seem to acquire respect. Even his friends begin to avoid him.

On the other hand, the congressman who consults privately with shrewdness, who has just come from a closed meeting with somebody with information to impart, who works quietly underground, will wind up in the donjon with the prize. He will, in the course of time, exert influence. He will be asked for his opinion. In a profession which makes much of handing out advice, it is being asked for it that is the greatest jewel.

People speculate and newspapermen occasionally complain about why the congressman doesn't speak out. He doesn't speak out because this is not the way to power. Power is in silence, in committee, in personal relations. If a frustrated congressman must speak out, he can do so in the Appendix of the *Congressional Record*. (This fascinating department furnishes the complete outlet for congressional feelings. Contents are limited only by the discretion of the individual.) If the congressman actually wishes to exercise his vocal cords as part of his therapy, he can talk to an empty House at the close of the regular business under another curious institution called "Special Orders."

There is another reason why speaking out in the House is not favored. It is because such public display is largely fruitless. The fact is that no one reports congressional debate.

The idea of the House as a forum for public expression is a huge fiction which should be recognized. Debate in the House is usually a shallow thing, difficult to follow, and it must be very difficult to report. Therefore, the press pays almost no attention to debate in the House. Reporters are where power is. They don't waste their valuable time in the House press gallery unless an important vote is to be taken. They are to be found in the Speaker's Lobby where the powerful are.

As I have indicated, reputations are seldom made in debate. But reputations can be lost by seeking the public way to power—in the open assault over the walls. Some congressmen are known as the "kiss of death" because their public display drives off votes. In one lively exchange, an urbane New Yorker asked a certain congressman to yield, and asked, "You are for my bill?" When the answer came in the affirmative, the New Yorker hurried up the aisle, his arms waving over his head in mock horror, symbolizing certain defeat. He lost, too.

It is a matter of the greatest interest how reputations are hung on a man. It goes to the nature of Congress, I suppose. The political relationship is at one and the same time intensely personal, and yet blandly impersonal. The typical congressman exudes personal friendship by the yard. Everyone is a bosom buddy from the word go—first names all over the place, affectionate grabs of arms and shoulders, pats and taps. A sick Member returning is the center of warm attention. Praise is bandied around in wholesale lots, and your first trips to this candy factory leave you feeling a little heavy.

Yet, this intense, clubby, personal relationship continually smacks with great force directly into the cold, cruel hardness of the vote. The close friend you were grimacing with not two minutes before votes with the other people. You may be able to shrug this off by rationalizing that "he's voting his district," but frequently it hurts. On certain key votes this effect is monstrous to such a degree that new alignments, stock-taking, etc., occur. "It's not only his neck," you speculate. "He's putting his/my party on the block. He's putting *me* on the block."

This alternation between the role of buddy and executioner, in greater or lesser degree, creates great strains that often become almost intolerable. That politicians have thick skins is simply not a reliable opinion. Politicians are usually in politics because they are "feeling" people. Their feelings toward one another are the most acute of all. Hence, a session of Congress is a wearing affair.

The result of these sharp-honed feelings is an enlarged apperception that is used to scrutinize fellow Members. While congressmen are quite ordinary in general outline, their practice of the political art has made them knowledgeable in assessing one another. Their instincts, sharpened by this conflict of the personal and the impersonal, enable them to characterize each other to the finest hair. Thus, each congressman is given his own little pigeonhole, with all his strengths and weaknesses, foibles and tricks, duly noted for use on the proper occasions. Power, then, is the respect which accrues and adheres to those individuals who are best able to stand this daily etching process.

Very sincerely,
Clem Miller

Dear Friend:

In recent weeks we have been talking about the locus of congressional power. Let us now relate it to the Floor of the House. Previously, we have seen that as an issue mounts in importance, ability to influence on the Floor of the House lessens.

We have also seen that debate changes few votes. Now let us consider how votes *are* changed. Members do change the votes of other Members and Members do switch from vote to vote. This is done on a personal basis. But shifts of this kind seldom change a final result. Final results are almost always changed only by a hierarchic shift. Even in these instances, substantial hierarchic changes can be made without immediately altering the final result. For example, the South is shifting from a pro-mutual security position to one opposed. There was a shift of thirty-four votes between 1958 and 1959. However, the influx of northern Democrats cancelled the effect this shift might otherwise have had.

Now, to understand the manner in which an individual might be induced to change his vote, let us first examine the seating arrangements in the House Chamber. Republicans arrange themselves on the Speaker's left, Democrats on his right. Attendance is a chancy affair. Democrats outnumber Republicans generally, but the latter are there when they have to be.

There are no assigned seats in the Chamber. There are characteristic groupings. Illinois always sits in a back corner. Massachusetts has a steady little knot in the center aisle. The southerners arrange themselves in a boot-shaped group behind the majority tables. Kentucky is a solid row, center aisle. And immediately behind them sit Brock and McGinley of Nebraska in what you might call the left-field bleachers. Connecticut sits together but the place changes from day to day. I could go blindfolded to the seats many Members habitually sit in. Others stand behind the rail, in the rear. Others stand along the sides, and never sit at all. Others walk in one door to respond to their names at roll calls and immediately exit by another. Others inhabit the cloakroom.

Then there are the floaters, going from group to group, taking soundings, reporting rumors. "How are you going to vote on the ———Bill?" The floaters link the sub-blocs to establish a consensus.

Let's see how this works out in practice. Let us refer to a bill relatively devoid of party overtones—for example, the Auto Safety Bill. Some representatives seemed to be against it because it might cost some money in the Department of Commerce. Other congressmen were for it because it promised to save lives, and thus, they argued, would save money in the long run. But by and large, there was doubt and hesitation. Everywhere the call was, "How are you going to vote?" State delegations sent representatives around to do private polling. No one appeared to be following the debate. There was banter back and forth. "Are you against *saving lives?*" "What are you, a *spender?*" Little knots of conversation, much of it seeming idle or irrelevant, actually signified a working out of opinions. The roll begins: "Abbitt, Abernathy, Adair, Addonizio. . . ." Some wait for bellwethers. They pass over the first call, listening for key votes.

I saw one influential Democrat listening to a friend who wants him to vote "no." He does so. Then, later, he taps another friend on the shoulder. "How'd you vote?" The other friend voted for it. Sheepishly, and amidst some kidding, "influential" gets up at the call's end to change his vote. A small incident, but this is the working out of power. "Another friend" has power because he was consulted by one with power.

The most interesting roll call of the session, in my mind, was on the so-called Vault Cash Bill. This was designed, among other things, to lower reserves of Federal Reserve member banks. It was regarded as a giveaway of billions by some. To others, it constituted a small but significant addition to inflation. To most, it was a confusing bill, almost incomprehensible and not very significant.

Some Members asked friends, "Is it a giveaway?" "No, but . . ." The floaters scurried back and forth. At the end, in frustrated confusion, many Members went with the committee chairman who had reported the bill favorably. The fact that it gave advantages to banks stirred the embers of the old Populist sentiment and fanned the sparks of a younger group. These congressmen were aroused and they were convinced on a personal basis. The leadership of the committee chairman was not persuasive to them. However, the tradition of following the chairman was strong enough to hold a majority to his side, so the revolt failed.

What may be learned from these examples is that voting lines are set by the committee chairmen (and by each committee's senior minority member) and hence by the Leadership; that generally this is sufficient to carry the day; and finally, that individuals may shift back and forth within this framework in response to personal appeals and deeply ingrained prejudices. The total effect is a series of decisions inspired by committee leaders, but lacking coordinated, overall policy direction.

Very sincerely,
Clem Miller

Dear Friend:

This is basically a report on power in the House of Representatives. It must be tentative, as all such things are.

As I see it, power in the House is a personal thing. A congressman accedes to power by his own personal actions over a period of time. Having said that, let me quickly contradict myself by saying that power is also hierarchical in nature. Power adheres to committee chairmen, and filters slowly down to the lower ranks.

As I have reported previously, Congress is a collection of committees that come together in a Chamber periodically to approve one another's actions. The committee chairman or ranking minority member becomes the rallying point for his party in any debate on any given bill. Unlike other deliberative bodies, the Floor Leader for a piece of legislation is the committee chairman rather than the Majority Leader.

Members will frequently, and even customarily, follow a committee chairman against their own best interests and against the dictates of friendship or reason. A case comes vividly to mind. On the Landrum-Griffin Bill the chairman of the committee had agreed with the Republicans to sacrifice what seemed to him a good amendment in order to get their approval on the overall bill, thus forestalling a bitter battle. A minority of us on the committee made a vigorous Floor fight on this amendment which we also regarded as desirable. The facts, the presentation, and the merits were all on the side of a "yes" vote. Yet, on a standing vote, a good share of the Democrats stood up with the chairman to say "nay," although we felt no case had been made.

Such loyalty to committee chairmen may undergo revision in

our next session. When the Landrum-Griffin Bill was up for vote, thirteen of the nineteen committee chairmen deserted the Speaker to favor the bill. This graphically illustrated the locus of power in the House. The Speaker, unable to deliver votes, was revealed in outline against the chairmen. This fact was not lost on Democratic Members. Last January the Speaker pledged that legislation would not be permitted to languish in committee or to be forestalled by the Rules Committee. The Landrum-Griffin Bill was mute evidence that this pledge could not be redeemed. Those who (with excellent hindsight) now criticize the agreement with the Speaker should be reminded that until the redemption of this pledge was made clear to all, no one could make a move.

The effect of this new appraisal may be detected in several unnoted votes after this time. For example, the Chairman of the Agriculture Committee opposed an amendment to an agricultural bill offered by a ranking Republican. He glanced around at the substantial Democratic membership arrayed behind him, but was dismayed to see seventy of them stand up with the Republican's forces to carry the amendent against the southern Democrats, 153–52.

Another interesting series of votes occurred on the second housing bill. The Republicans proposed a series of limiting amendments. The southerners bounced up about forty strong to vote with the Republicans for the first amendment on a teller, pass-through count. The hostility on the part of other Democrats to this action was as visible as an unsheathed knife. Then, as each amendment came along fewer southerners arose with the Republicans, till at last there were only five left, conspicuously self-conscious.

If these are portents for the next session, and well they might be, chairmen will not be so successful in securing the automatic allegiance of their junior colleagues. This could mean some shift of power.

It is more likely, however, that any coalition of northern forces will have only limited success. Congressional government, by the design of our forefathers, does not encourage coordinate political action. A coalition of northerners, without interior lines of strength, is a tenuous thing. The very reason many are here is that they tend to be individualistic, hence not readily amenable to central authority. There is no unifying philosophy such as the issue of segregation is to the southerners. While northern Democrats have generally similar objectives, on any given vote there is enough disagreement among them to result in noticeable defection and frequent defeat.

Let us return to the analogy with warfare. The committees with their chairmen are like a string of forts. The northern coalition, as the attackers, are spread out, with poor communication and hence poor coordination. They have no base of power from which to menace the chairmen on the one hand, or to discipline their members on the other.

The greatest hazard to the besiegers, however, is the undependability of their coalition. They may have determined a strategy, only to discover that one of the barons has left the line with his levies to return home, or to sue for a separate peace with the defenders. Certain significant blocs of votes owe their primary and definitive allegiance to their city or state, and the outlines of broad policy always give way before local needs.

A graphic example comes to mind. On the vote to override Eisenhower's second public works veto, one leader who controlled four other votes on this issue held those votes out till the end. The vote was very close. We could all see him negotiating about something with the Majority Leader near the Speaker's rostrum. Finally, the bloc's votes were recorded in favor of the override. The results of the negotiations are not known to me. Perhaps it was a tour de force. But the lesson was there. If a leader were willing to jeopardize his party on such a major test of strength, it is not hard to see how much more this is true in lesser but still significant matters.

Very sincerely,
Clem Miller

Dear Friend:

This is the legislative time of year for the "conference" committee, the "conference" report, and thus, the season for final passage of the bills which have been in process since the opening days of the session. The conference is the little-known device by which differences between the House version of a bill and its Senate counterpart are worked out. Each body, House and Senate, appoints conferees. There may be four or eight or nine, with representation from the Republican and Democratic sides, proportioned to their relative strength in the whole membership.

Conference committees make their own rules. The watchword is informality. Committee meetings are bargaining sessions between principals who know the game. The preliminaries are out of the way. Now is the time to hammer out the finished product.

Presumably the conference has the duty of resolving, by compromise, the differences between House and Senate. If all goes well, this is achieved. The resultant bill, identical to the last comma, is returned to each house. No amendment is possible, accept or reject. Almost always the conference report is adopted. If things do not go so well, and agreement seems impossible, conferees return to their respective houses to ask for "instructions." At the same time, the conferees "suggest" that we recede on this point, stand fast there, agree on another. Our concurrence is readily had. Armed with these "instructions," the conferees return to the battle until all-encompassing agreement is reached. Should no agreement be possible, the bill is dead.

In actual practice, the conference report is far more than a compromise between the houses. Very frequently it is a goal, a haven for legislative policy. It is a rare House chairman who pilots his bill through the House without keeping at least one eye on the conference which will almost certainly result, for rarely does an important bill exactly conform to the companion bill in the Senate. When he so affably makes points with a Member by adopting his pet amendment, the chairman knows he can recede gracefully from it in conference. He may adopt a very weak or a very strong position on a certain issue to put himself in a better bargaining position at the conference. The larger the bag of tricks a chairman takes to conference, the more free play he has in the negotiation. For, though a conference is supposed to be a *resolution* of differences, the finished product is frequently a strange mélange of the original ingredients plus others not so easily defined.

We can draw some grim amusement from the loud hurly-burly which accompanies a bill through its initial stages, the countless hours of haggling in committee and on the Floor—for a comma or an adjective—and then observe the whole business disappear, swallowed up in a conference report.

There are good reasons for the phenomenon of bone-bruising Floor battles usually culminating in tranquil conference committee love affairs. The conference committee is the ultimate flowering of the power of seniority. For those who have followed these newsletters from the beginning I have sought to trace the interplay of forces at work here. There is cooperation. There is contention: the ins vs. the outs, the old boys vs. the new boys. Through it all we have been trying to perceive the locus of power.

The conference committee is the central core of the power. The Speaker's authority to appoint conferees is one of his most important prerogatives. He selects as members of the conference committee the senior members of the standing committee originating the legislation. He appoints the Democrats and Republicans. The conference committee meets in secret. No one who is not privy to the conference committee knows its workings. Away from prying eyes, any display of partisanship can be easily shed, as the comrades in arms from both sides recognize a mutuality of interest, and at the same time they may reaffirm the importance of seniority, the control of senior members. This is not to say there are no crushing conference committee battles. There are. But it takes a really big issue to disrupt the conference with an open battle.

This suggests another major function of the legislative process— synthesis, or perhaps a better word, distillation. Issues are synthesized, distilled. At each stage the pressures to conform are greater. At each stage the partisan issue must be a large one to survive. At the conference stage most of the partisanship has been wrung out, and what remains is the seniors vs. the rest, the seniors in both parties who preside uneasily over the roiling mass below.

There are exceptions and, like most exceptions, they prove the rule. The School Bill passed the House last year, and the Rules Committee, in a fit of rebellion, refused to report out a Rule on appointment of conferees. The Speaker appoints conferees, but he does it with a Rule from the Rules Committee. The committee would not grant one on this important bill. While there were other reasons, it was also defiance and a demonstration of power. What should be noted, however, is the fact that the committee does not press this advantage too often. Wisely, the members, seniors all, realize that its exercise threatens seniority. Power exercised too often outside the regular order is power dissipated.

Very sincerely,
Clem Miller

Policy Effects of the Two-Year Term

Charles O. Jones

The political adage that tinkering with rules is tampering with policy is borne out dramatically in any analysis of the proposal that members of the House of Representatives be elected for four-year terms. The most recent proponent was President Johnson, whose mere mention of the idea in his 1966 State of the Union address brought sustained, enthusiastic applause. In a special message, the President stated, "We have learned that brief and uncertain periods in office contribute—not to the best interests of democracy—but to harassed inefficiency and the loss of invaluable experience." He spoke of the increased volume of legislation in recent years and the difficulty of conducting political campaigns when the pressures of the work load virtually mean year-round sessions. He went on to underscore the complexity

SOURCE: Charles O. Jones, *Every Second Year: Congressional Behavior and the Two-Year Term* (Washington, D.C.: The Brookings Institution, 1967), ch. 4, pp. 72–95 (tables have been renumbered). Reprinted with permission. Many of the author's impressions came from a series of round-table discussions at Brookings in which eighteen Congressmen and twelve congressional staff members participated.

and diversity of modern legislation and the frustrations members suffer as they try to meet their legislative responsibilities while conducting biennial campaigns. And he dwelt on the increasing costs of political campaigning, noting that the enormous expenditures often prevented otherwise qualified persons from becoming candidates.

These were the stated reasons, and while they merit serious consideration, there are even more significant factors, though they are less likely to find their way into presidential messages or floor debates. The four-year term has a special attraction for those who believe that American government functions most successfully when the initiative is with the President. Under the present system of two-year terms, the voting turnout for off-year elections is lower than in presidential years, those elections are much more likely to be dominated by local issues and personalities, and the party in power invariably loses seats. For example, if we take the off-year elections since 1922, the party in power lost an average of forty-one House seats (the only exception being 1934, when the Democrats gained nine House seats). Such losses mean a swift falling off of support for presidential programs, as Professor Charles O. Jones demonstrates in the selection reprinted below.

Despite the initial enthusiasm for President Johnson's suggestion, the proposal has been pigeonholed, again for reasons that are not frequently or candidly spelled out. The fact is that the present system has not been unkind to very many House members.

Most states have apportioned their congressional districts in such a manner that there are very few genuine contests, that is, districts where a winner receives less than 55 percent of the vote. In 1966, for example, nearly eight out of ten members of the House came from safe districts. In an analysis of House elections between 1952 and 1960, Professors William J. Keefe and Morris S. Ogul have noted that ". . . it would have been possible to have had 1,740 changes (435 × 4), an indication of perfect competitiveness. Actual changes numbered only 135 or 7.8 percent. Viewed broadly, the chances are that the same party will win five consecutive elections in about three-fourths of all congressional districts." This simply means that most members of the House are not really running for office; they are standing for election. So why change a system that may only add perils without rewards?

Two other factors cloud the recent discussions of this problem. There is no doubt that the decrease in presidential popularity in 1967 and 1968 damaged the likelihood that any proposal to strengthen the Executive branch would be viewed sympathetically. Indeed, the vast use of presidential prerogatives during the Vietnam War compelled many liberals to reexamine their traditional faith in a strong Presidency. Moreover, many politicians and political scientists also contended that, with all of its limitations, the midterm election is a useful if inexact referendum on national issues and therefore a vital part of representative government.

The two-year term will be a fact of political life for years to come. A full understanding of its premises and its consequences is at the same time an invaluable insight into the fragile, sensitive world of executive–legislative relationships.

All proponents of the four-year term express concern over the effects of the two-year term on policy-making. Those who favor having the members run with the President are concerned about the effect of the off-year election on the presidential program. A president deserves to have a majority on which he can rely, they say, and "divided responsibility should be avoided." Mid-term elections can divide the executive from Congress. Also, the two-year term leaves the member with too little time for studying public problems and legislation. A four-year term would relieve him of the continual burden of campaigning, so that he and his staff could spend more time on legislative tasks. And a longer term would encourage the House to tackle more controversial issues, since the number of elections would be reduced.

The advocates of a staggered four-year term, on the other hand, agree that the latter two effects exist, but they do not wish to give the President any more power over Congress than he already has. Thus, they are not persuaded that all members should run with the President. The two-year termers simply reject all three assertions.

Several sets of data will be examined in this chapter so as to determine what are, in fact, the policy effects of the two-year term. Four problems will be examined: House support for presidential programs, the extent to which controversial legislation is avoided, how the member allocates his time, and what the staff does.

Congressional Support of Presidential Programs

The first evidence to set forth is that on the frequency of party division between Congress and the presidency. How often has the President lost control of Congress during the mid-term elections? During presidential elections? How often has his party's margin been reduced in mid-term elections? During presidential elections? How often has his party's margin been increased? Table 1 presents those data for this century.[1]

There is ample support for the conclusion that the President is more likely to have a majority from his own party in Congress when members run with him. Only once in this century has the President's party increased its margin in both houses during a mid-term election, whereas in nine of the sixteen presidential election years, the President's party has increased its margin in both houses. Conversely, the President's party has had its margin reduced in both houses in thirteen of the seventeen mid-term elections and in only two of the sixteen presidential year elections. The President has never lost control of both houses in a presidential election year in this century, though in 1956 President Eisenhower failed to regain control of Congress after it had been lost to the Democrats in 1954. There is a clear advantage to the President's party in Congress dur-

[1] See American Enterprise Institute, "Proposals for 4-Year Terms for Members of the House of Representatives," Feb. 18, 1966, pp. 18–19.

TABLE 1

SUCCESS OF PRESIDENT'S PARTY IN CONGRESSIONAL ELECTIONS, 1900–66[a]

Election year	Margin of President's party	
	In the Senate	In the House
Presidential election year		
1900	Remained the same	Increased
1904	Remained the same	Increased
1908	Decreased	Decreased
1912	Increased	Increased
1916	Decreased	Decreased
1920	Increased	Increased
1924	Increased	Increased
1928	Increased	Increased
1932	Increased	Increased
1936	Increased	Increased
1940	Decreased	Increased
1944	Remained the same	Increased
1948	Increased	Increased
1952	Increased	Increased
1956	Remained the same	Decreased
1960	Increased	Increased
1964	Remained the same	Increased
Mid-term election year		
1902	Decreased	Decreased
1906	Increased	Decreased
1910	Decreased	Decreased[b]
1914	Increased	Decreased
1918	Decreased[c]	Decreased[c]
1922	Decreased	Decreased
1926	Decreased	Decreased
1930	Decreased	Decreased
1934	Increased	Increased
1938	Decreased	Decreased
1942	Decreased	Decreased
1946	Decreased[c]	Decreased[c]
1950	Decreased	Decreased
1954	Decreased[c]	Decreased[c]
1958	Decreased	Decreased
1962	Increased	Decreased
1966	Decreased	Decreased

[a] Changes are measured by the number of members a party had after each election. Changes which may have occurred between elections are not accounted for.

[b] President's party lost control of the House of Representatives.

[c] President's party lost control of Congress.

SOURCE: *Congress and the Nation, 1945–1964* (Congressional Quarterly Service, 1965).

ing the presidential election years (although not necessarily attributable to the coattail effect).[2]

A greater margin in Congress for the President's party does not translate directly into greater presidential support. The next evidence to examine, therefore, is the extent to which the President receives support for his program from Congresses elected at different times. The *Congressional Quarterly* has been compiling comparative presidential support scores and box scores on legislation since the 83rd Congress, in 1952. These data are pertinent to the present problem. Seven Congresses have been elected since 1952—four during presidential election years and three during mid-term election years.

First, it is necessary to determine how well the President does with Congress. The *Congressional Quarterly* has two methods for determining this—the President's legislative box score (the percentage of his requests enacted into law), and the percentage of roll calls won by the President (that is, where he has taken a stand in favor or against). Table 2 indicates the President's scores by these two measures, 1953–66. There is additional evidence here to support the case of the four-year-term proponents. The mean box score for all presidential requests during Congresses elected with him is 54.5 percent, compared with 39.8 percent during Congresses elected in the mid-term. The mean presidential support score for all roll calls during Congresses elected with the President is 82.4 percent, compared with 73 percent for Congresses elected in the mid-term. Thus, during this time period Congress generally provided the President with more support during the first two years of his administration.

If the Eisenhower administration and the Kennedy-Johnson administrations are examined separately, however, the generalization

[2] See Warren E. Miller, "Political Coattails: A Study in Political Myth and Methodology," *Public Opinion Quarterly*, Vol. 19 (Winter 1955–56), pp. 352–68; Malcolm Moos, *Politics, Presidents, and Coattails* (Baltimore, Md.: Johns Hopkins Press, 1952); and Angus Campbell and Warren E. Miller, "The Motivational Basis of Straight and Split Ticket Voting," *American Political Science Review*, Vol. 51 (June, 1957), pp. 293–312.

TABLE 2

PRESIDENTIAL SCORES WITH CONGRESS, 1953–66

Congress	Legislative requests			Roll calls		
	Total number	Number enacted	Percent- age enacted	Total number	Number won	Percent- age won
Presidential Congresses						
83d, 1st sess. (1953)	44	32	*72.7*	83	74	*89.2*
83d, 2d sess. (1954)	232	150	*64.7*	115	90	*78.3*
85th, 1st sess. (1957)	206	76	*36.9*	117	80	*68.4*
85th, 2d sess. (1958)	234	110	*47.0*	148	112	*75.7*
87th, 1st sess. (1961)	355	172	*48.4*	189	154	*81.5*
87th, 2d sess. (1962)	298	133	*44.6*	185	158	*85.4*
89th, 1st sess. (1965)	469	323	*68.9*	274	255	*93.1*
89th, 2d sess. (1966)	371	207	*55.8*	228	180	*79.0*
Total	2209	1203	*54.5*	1339	1103	*82.4*
Mid-term Congresses						
84th, 1st sess. (1955)	207	96	*46.3*	93	70	*75.3*
84th, 2d sess. (1956)	225	103	*45.7*	99	69	*69.7*
86th, 1st sess. (1959)	228	93	*40.8*	175	91	*52.0*
86th, 2d sess. (1960)	183	56	*30.6*	129	84	*65.1*
88th, 1st sess. (1963)	401	109	*27.2*	186	162	*87.1*
88th, 2d sess. (1964)	217	125	*57.6*	149	131	*87.9*
Total	1461	582	*39.8*	831	607	*73.0*

SOURCE: Compiled from data in *Congressional Quarterly Almanacs* for relevant years.

is modified somewhat. Rather sizable differences continue to exist between presidential box scores for presidential Congresses and mid-term Congresses for both administrations (see Table 3). Based

TABLE 3

AVERAGE PRESIDENTIAL SCORES WITH CONGRESS, EISENHOWER
AND KENNEDY-JOHNSON ADMINISTRATIONS

		Eisenhower		Kennedy-Johnson	
		Presidential Congresses	Mid-term Congresses	Presidential Congresses	Mid-term Congresses
$\bar{x}$	Box Score	51.4	41.3	55.9	37.9
$\bar{x}$	Presidential Support Score	76.9	63.3	85.3	87.5

SOURCE: Compiled from data in *Congressional Quarterly Almanacs.*

on these very limited data, it appears that the President has considerably more difficulty getting his requests through mid-term Congresses. Having gotten a bill to the roll call stage, however, Presidents Kennedy and Johnson were equally successful in winning majorities in both presidential and mid-term Congresses. As noted in Table 3, Kennedy-Johnson had an average presidential support score of 85.3 during presidential Congresses and a remarkably high average support score of 87.5 during mid-term Congresses. President Eisenhower had much less success with support scores during his mid-term Congresses (13.6 less than in presidential Congresses).

What was the source of the difficulty for President Eisenhower? The principal problem was that too many Democrats were elected during the mid-term elections. His own party continued to support him at the same level as during presidential Congresses (see Table 4), but two trends cut into his congressional support—more Democrats were elected, *and* the average support score for Democratic

TABLE 4

HOUSE PRESIDENTIAL SUPPORT SCORES BY PARTY, 1954–66

Congress and date	President's party		Opposition party	
	Presidential Congresses	Mid-term Congresses	Presidential Congresses	Mid-term Congresses
83d 1954	71		44	
84th 1955		60		53
1956		72		52
85th 1957	54		49	
1958	58		55	
86th 1959		68		40
1960		59		44
87th 1961	73		37	
1962	72		42	
88th 1963		72		32
1964		74		38
89th 1965	74		41	
1966	63		37	

SOURCE: Compiled from data in *Congressional Quarterly Almanacs*.

congressmen went down. During the Kennedy-Johnson administrations, Democrats were able to maintain large majorities (at least until 1966) and high presidential support scores.

Thus, it appears that the two-year term can very definitely have an effect on the presidential program. Important differences in congressional support of the President between presidential Congresses and mid-term Congresses can develop. The biennial elections are particularly troublesome for a minority party President (Eisenhower) since if he has a majority in Congress at all, it is likely to be a very small one. There is a high probability, therefore, that the expected loss of seats for the presidential party in Congress during mid-term elections will result in the loss of control of Congress. A majority party President, on the other hand, will probably bring with him a large majority in Congress and therefore he does not face quite the same mid-term election problem as the minority party President. There are further difficulties of analysis, however. The legislative box score for President Kennedy in 1963 (see Table 2) was the lowest of any during the period measured. At the same time it should be noted that Kennedy made many more requests than Eisenhower had ever made, and that many of these requests were enacted into law in later sessions.[3]

The proponents of concurrent four-year terms, with the President, do have evidence in support of their contentions. Even where there is no decline in presidential support following biennial elections, it is obvious that the potential of creating an anti-administration Congress is always present. It may well be that there would be a decline in presidential support during the last two years of an administration anyway, but it seems much less likely if the same majority is to serve throughout the four years than if changes are made.

This evidence can also be used to support the arguments of the short-termers and those who fear the staggered and off-year proposals. They would argue that any decrease in presidential support which comes from a loss of seats by the presidential party or a change in attitude by presidential party members following the mid-term is perfectly in order. Indeed, that is the purpose of the mid-term election. One Republican round-table participant even made this point about his own administration:

After the Republican Congress came in it lasted only two years and then the people had a chance to express themselves and voted the Republicans out. This off-year national referendum which is in effect a measure of the public sentiment about the administration, I think, is a very valuable thing.

[3] This point raises some question about the usefulness of these scores. A President may have high scores because he proposes only what he thinks Congress will pass—regardless of whether the problem is solved or not. Another President may score low because he is supporting innovative solutions which later are accepted after he leaves the White House.

Once again, it should be emphasized that vastly different interpretations of the job of a representative and executive-legislative relations influence the reactions of these groups to various aspects of the length-of-term issue. There are definite negative policy effects for the President in the two-year term. Whether they are "adverse" or not is debatable.

Controversial Legislation

Another argument for a longer term is that House members would be less hesitant to act on controversial legislation because elections would be less frequent. With elections occurring every two years, it is asserted, such legislation is shelved because members do not want to go on record as favoring or opposing. Presumably this is legislation which results in conflicts for the congressmen, since they believe that constituents are divided on the issue. Voting either way would, in the member's analysis, lose him votes. Thus, he prefers to avoid recording himself one way or the other.

If true, the argument above is a persuasive one in favor of a longer term. Certainly, the four-year term would not completely eliminate any such phenomenon; only reduce its frequency. As one member noted, "Give us a year. The fourth year is still a tough one." But even reducing the avoidance of legislative action because a bill is controversial seems to be an attractive reason for change.

What is the record on this matter? Does the House avoid controversial legislation during election years? As with so many assertions by the long-term proponents, hard evidence is uncommonly difficult to collect. Individual members can cite legislation which, in their opinion, has been shelved because of election-year politics. Several did so during round-table discussions. It is true that controversial legislation often is not acted on in election years. But what is in question is the extent to which such legislation is not acted on in election years, contrasted with nonelection years.

It should also be possible to identify, as the cause for nonaction, the fact that members do not wish to record themselves because of election-year politics.

Table 5 presents the percentages of presidential legislative pro-

TABLE 5

PRESIDENTIAL REQUESTS ACCEPTED OR REJECTED, 1953–66[a]

Congress	Nonelection year	Election year
83d	1953—79.5%	1954—85.8%
84th	1955—54.1	1956—62.7
85th	1957—48.1	1958—71.8
86th	1959—61.8	1960—53.0
87th	1961—66.8	1962—60.1
88th	1963—42.6	1964—64.1
89th	1965—80.6	1966—75.7

[a] Includes all bills rejected in committee or on the floor of either house.
SOURCE: *Congressional Quarterly Almanacs.*

posals (presumably the major source of controversial legislation) which were either accepted or rejected by Congress, 1953–66, divided into election and nonelection years. Given the assertion above, it would be logical to expect that Congress would put itself on record less during election years. In fact, the percentages are greater for election years in four of the seven Congresses where the figures are available for both sessions—the reverse of what one might expect. Overall, 68.4 percent of all presidential proposals during the election years measured were either accepted or rejected; 61.4 percent were either accepted or rejected during nonelection years. Thus, this type of gross analysis of presidential proposals fails to provide any proof of the assertion that controversial legislation is avoided during election years. In fact, the figures seem to indicate that many measures are held over from the first to the second session before final action is taken—perhaps because they are complex and controversial.

It may be that those presidential proposals which do not receive final action in election years are controversial, while those which do not receive final action in nonelection years are not controversial. Any proof of this conclusion would depend on one's judgment as to what is controversial legislation. If such legislation is defined as being of national importance, having widespread effect, and characterized by opposing interests, then it does not seem that the conclusion can be supported by the evidence. A review of specific legislation which did not receive final action by Congress during the years 1962 to 1965 simply does not support the proposition that controversial legislation is avoided in election years.[4] Many of the major controversial proposals which were neither passed nor defeated in those years were "hardy perennials." Such measures as federal aid to education, medical care for the aged, civil defense, area redevelopment, minimum wage, labor legislation of various types, were shelved *both* in election years and non-election years. They were not acted on because many of the issues could not be resolved satisfactorily to all of the interests involved.

Perhaps the President does not propose controversial legislation during election years and does in nonelection years. That assertion, while perfectly logical, makes a different point from that set forth by the long-term proponents. Congress is not avoiding legislation if legislation is not proposed in the first place. It is probably true that the President will try to capitalize on his electoral victory in the first year of his presidency and introduce a wide variety of measures—particularly if his majority is as large as Lyndon B. Johnson's in 1964. But he will likely do that anyway; regardless of whether House members are elected for a two- or four-year term.

In conclusion, it is no doubt true that the House does not act on certain controversial measures during an election year because

[4] The *Congressional Quarterly* has, since 1962, included sections on "What Congress Did Not Do" in the year-end *Almanac*. The conclusions in this paragraph are based on an examination of those policy issues.

certain members are concerned about making a record which could conceivably hurt them. Indeed, round-table participants gave examples of legislation which, in their opinion, was held up for these reasons. The problem becomes one of proving that the practice exists to such an extent that it is necessary to change the length of term for House members. A hunch is not enough to prove the case. And even where one can demonstrate that the practice exists, with specific examples, one can also point to cases which upset the generalization. Thus, in 1966, the "situs picketing" bill was given as an example, by round-table participants, of a bill which was too "hot" to be voted on. But, on the other hand, the House spent over a week in 1966 debating, revising, and voting on a major civil rights bill—the third major civil rights bill in three years.

The Time Problem

There is another policy-related argument in support of a longer term—that the member would have more time to devote to considering various alternative solutions to public problems. Freed from at least one set of campaigns, the argument goes, the member could turn his attention to legislative duties, and the result would be beneficial for the nation. But how do members allocate their time now? And what are they likely to do with whatever extra time they would have from a longer term?

The first point to make is, of course, that the allocation of time by a representative will depend upon a number of factors. The committee assignment of the member may be important. Membership on certain committees, notably Ways and Means and Appropriations, may be time consuming. Other committees have more limited responsibilities. The member's seniority and leadership post, if any, may determine in part how he allocates his time. Other factors of importance may include the various political, economic, and geographical characteristics of the constituency. [For example], not every member has a tightly contested primary and general election to engage his attention. Thus, some members have more time to devote to legislation than others because of the political situation in the district. Districts also differ considerably in terms of economic problems which require the attention of the member. Geographical considerations also play a role. Those districts in the East which are near Washington (particularly those in nearby Maryland and Virginia; many of whose constituents phone in their problems) require constant servicing by their members. On the other hand, Far West districts require lengthy travel time on the part of the member. And obviously, during the election year, the member with an opponent must focus his attention on the district. If he faces a stiff challenge, the member, and his staff, may be completely preoccupied with reelection activities.

There are many other possible determinants of how a man allocates his time—e.g., temper of the times, whether his party controls the White House and Congress, pressure group activity —but perhaps the most important of all is how the member views the job. Several colloquies developed during the round-table discussions between members who took opposing views on how a representative should spend his time. The principal disagreement was on how much time ought to be spent on constituency service:

CONGRESSMAN A: [Congressman B], as much as I love you, I find myself in very substantial disagreement with you. I just do not agree that that particular activity is the primary function of a legislator.

CONGRESSMAN B: Which activity? I said there were two primary activities.

CONGRESSMAN A: You referred to one about the contact with the constituents, the so-called running of errands . . . I don't think that is one of our primary functions.

CONGRESSMAN B: Then we do disagree.

CONGRESSMAN C: I don't know how I can be a better legislator if someone wants me to get him out of the armed services or a promotion or get him a transfer or other problems that they come to me with that have nothing to do with legislation. I don't see how it makes me a better legislator. It doesn't give me any idea of what they are thinking about, whether a piece of legislation is good or bad or indifferent.

CONGRESSMAN B: [Congressman C], you are assuming by this last argument that the congressman's job is solely that of a legislator, and I insist that a congressman's job is not that of a legislator only. It is a two-pronged job. He is a representative of his people, not only in terms of representing them in legislation, but in terms of representing them in the executive branch.

CONGRESSMAN C: You are destroying the concept of division of authority between the legislature, judiciary, and executive.

This colloquy well illustrates the difference between those members who think that it is important to concentrate on legislation and those who think that it is important to combine that effort with constituency service. Both types of members are basically oriented toward legislative functions—they only differ on methods. But there are other types of members too—those who are playing to a different audience and are less oriented toward legislative functions. First, there are those who view their service in Congress as being temporary. They are anxious to move elsewhere. Membership in Congress is a means to an end. One roundtable participant was particularly upset about those who are seeking national office. "They are misusing their positions, just like Bobby Kennedy going abroad when the Senate is in session. These are not the work horses in the legislative process."

Second, there are those who continuously campaign for re-election whether they need to or not. There are cases of members who "over-communicate" with and "over-solicit" the constituency to such an extent that they never have time to legislate. Indeed, as one staff member noted, some members generate constituency service matters and other trivia so that they will have an excuse for not legislating. How many legislators work hard to represent their districts in the legislative process, in the classical model of the district-oriented representative? One member who strongly subscribes to the model gave his assessment:

Increasingly fewer, but I would say surprisingly (maybe I can't use that adjective because I don't know what people anticipate; I base it on how many of my 435 colleagues are students) many. I give them a pretty good billing. *I would say about half.* I would say there are over a hundred damned good students in the Congress.

The member's interpretation of his responsibilities, therefore, becomes very important in determining how he will use his time. There is no "boss" to define his job for him.

How do most members use their time? This is an exceedingly difficult question to answer, since, apparently, no careful time-study has been done on Congress. One thing is certain: House members do not spend a great deal of time on the House floor; they are in committee meetings, or otherwise engaged.

One of the conditions which presumably makes the four-year term essential is that congressional sessions are longer now.

There have been long sessions in recent years, as there were during the immediate post-World War II years, but the average number of hours in session has varied little since 1947 (see Table 6). Since 1960, the House has been in session for an average of 160 days a year and 620 hours a year, for an average day of 3.9 hours. The Senate normally is in session more often than the House and the average day is longer. Assuming that there are 250 working days in a year (excluding weekends and holidays) and further assuming that the member gets 30 additional days' vacation, that still leaves the member 60 days (again excluding weekends and holidays) for campaigning if the House is in session for 160 days. And if the member works an eight-hour day, he has considerable time for legislative, committee, and constituency work, since the House is in session only half of that time and he will normally go to the House floor only when his presence there is required. Proponents of the four-year term would point out, however, that the number of days that the House is in session does not provide an accurate indication of the problem. The House does not stay in session the first 160 working days of the year and adjourn in August. When it is in session for 160 days, it generally does not adjourn until October or perhaps even later. Thus, campaigning

TABLE 6

TIME IN SESSION, 1947–64

Year	House			Senate		
	Days in session	Hours in session	Hours in average day	Days in session	Hours in session	Hours in average day
1947	144	686	4.8	143	808	5.7
1948	110	538	4.9	114	654	5.7
1949	165	704	4.3	186	1,145	6.2
1950	180	797	4.4	203	1,265	6.2
1951	163	705	4.3	172	997	5.8
1952	111	458	4.1	115	651	5.7
1953	117	507	4.3	125	764	6.1
1954	123	526	4.3	169	1,198	7.1
1955	112	471	4.2	105	560	5.3
1956	118	466	4.0	119	802	6.7
1957	141	585	4.2	133	861	6.5
1958	135	562	4.2	138	1,015	7.4
1959	141	527	3.7	140	1,010	7.2
1960	124	512	4.1	140	1,188	8.5
1961	147	570	3.9	146	1,005	6.9
1962	157	657	4.2	177	1,159	6.6
1963	186	626	3.7	189	1,045	5.5
1964	148	625	4.2	186	1,350	7.3

SOURCE: "Daily Digests" of various volumes of the *Congressional Record*.

has to be worked into the schedule of other duties. Blocks of time for campaigning, or for contemplating, are simply not available when the House is in session for long periods of time.

Davidson, Kovenock, and O'Leary asked the members they interviewed to name their most time-consuming activity and important secondary activities. The results are included in Table 7. Note that only 3 percent listed "campaigning" as a major activity, and 14 percent listed it as a secondary activity. But if "campaigning" is defined more broadly, to include case work, errands,

TABLE 7

MAJOR TIME-CONSUMING ACTIVITIES OF MEMBERS
OF THE HOUSE OF REPRESENTATIVES

Type of activity	Major time-consuming activity	Important as secondary activity
Legislation, committee work	77%	20%
Casework, "errands" for constituents	16	58
Publicity, communication with district	3	38
Campaigning	3	14
Intra-House politics	1	10
Washington social life	0	4
	100%	144%[a]

[a] The sum of the percentages of secondary activities exceeds 100 percent because a number of members mentioned more than one such activity.
SOURCE: U.S. Congress, Committee on Judiciary, Subcommittee No. 5, *Hearings*, "Congressional Tenure of Office," 89th Cong., 1st and 2d sess. (1965–66), p. 296.

communication with the district, then the percentages are increased considerably. These broadly defined campaign activities are particularly important as secondary work for the member. Would this be likely to change with a longer term? Davidson *et al.* do not think so:

. . . there is no assurance that longer terms would lighten these burdens perceptibly. Constituency service and communications are not, by and large, regulated by the proximity of elections. There is no reason to think that Senators have proportionately less constituency work because they enjoy 6-year rather than 2-year terms. . . . The essential point . . . is that a very large portion of constituency-related tasks are not bound up in the frequency of elections.[5]

[5] U.S. Cong., House, Committee on the Judiciary, Subcommittee No. 5, "Congressional Tenure of Office," 89th Cong., 1st and 2d sess. (1965–66), p. 297.

What would the member do with the extra time, if it material-
ized, of the longer term? The assumption of the long-termers is,
of course, that he would work on public problems so as to become
a better legislator. The members discussed this question in roundtables:

CONGRESSMAN A: I think it would not affect it because the nature of
a person [determines whether he] is going to be a student and be responsible and show energy and initiative. It will be the same whether
he is in for four years or two years. You [Congressman C] wouldn't
act any differently in a four-year term.

CONGRESSMAN B: He would get lazier and he knows it. We all would.
We would get lazier.

CONGRESSMAN C: I would not be doing the kind of thing that I think
is the most fruitful in getting knowledge and that is building up this
relationship with the constituency.

Other members were convinced that the additional time would
be devoted to public problems and their solutions—that the demands created by the present system simply prevent adequate
consideration of legislative problems. One member candidly remarked that he would "probably take trips and I am not sure the
taxpayer ought to have to pay for that."

Several conclusions can be set forth as a result of analyzing the
limited data available on this subject. First and foremost, how a
member allocates his time depends on a number of variables
aside from the length of his term. Particularly important is his
view of the job. Constituency-oriented members will probably
not change the manner in which they use their time if given a
longer term unless they change their interpretation of their responsibilities as well. "Constant campaigner" types will probably
continue with the same sorts of activities as before. Second, it
does appear that the House could arrange its business so as to use
time more efficiently. They stretch their days in session over a
long period of time and the average time in session on any one
day is rather low. It is interesting to note that the Joint Commit-

tee on the Organization of Congress made recommendations on this problem.[6] Third, members now apparently spend most of their time on legislation; what the increment would be if there were a four-year term is almost impossible to determine.

The Staff Problem

Closely related to the problem of how the member allocates his time is how staff time is allocated. There are three major staff activities: constituency service (usually called "case work"), campaign work, and legislative work. Obviously, these activities overlap and thus it is difficult to provide precise definition of what each includes. In his study of congressional staffs, Warren H. Butler does offer some general description of the service and legislative functions which are serviceable, however:

The service function encompasses all of the myriad demands for assistance and requests for information from private citizens and public officials that flow into the Member's office from the State or district every day. The legislative function includes obtaining the views of constituents and expressing the Member's own as an elected representative, the initiation of ideas within the legislative process, the evaluation of legislative proposals, and the review of the consequences as well as the administration of the laws.[7]

Campaign work would include those activities which are more directly related to the reelection of the member: getting nominating petitions, speechwriting for campaigns, scheduling cam-

---

[6] See U.S. Cong., Senate, Joint Committee on the Organization of Congress, "Organization of Congress," 89th Cong., 2d sess. (1966), Report No. 1414, p. 55.

[7] Warren H. Butler, "Administering Congress: The Role of the Staff," *Public Administration Review,* Vol. 26 (March, 1966), p. 3. See also Kenneth T. Kofmehl, *Professional Staffs of Congress* (Lafayette, Ind.: Purdue University Press, 1962). Unfortunately there is only a very limited amount of information in Kofmehl about personal staffs.

paign time, making arrangements in the district for campaign activities, sending out campaign literature, organizing, etc.

The member has a number of staff services at his disposal. For constituency-service work, he can rely on his own personal staff (which will vary from three to a maximum of eleven, with most at six or seven), the Legislative Reference Service, the bureaucracy, and, to a lesser extent, standing committee staffs. For campaign work he has to rely almost exclusively on his own staff, and party committee staffs, though he may get some indirect assistance from other staffs. For legislative work, he can rely on his staff, standing committee staffs (though there are problems, particularly for the minority, in getting assistance from staff who are appointed by senior members), the Legislative Reference Service, and the Legislative Counsel.[8]

Though there are a number of factors which are important in determining staff use (principally constituency characteristics and the member's view of his job),[9] all staffs spend most of their time on constituency-related problems. Campaign work and legislative work vary considerably office-to-office but the case load is high in practically every office. All of the round-table participants shared this conclusion. Some of their comments were:

The principal job of the staff is to handle the mail and to answer these inquiries. . . . Obviously you can't sit in committee all morning and be on the floor all afternoon and answer 100 letters a day. Somebody has to be back there tending to all of that. I think that is the real duty of a staff. If it does a job right, you get reelected.

•

I have one person who does legislative research work part of the time and I have six people that I call my communications link with my constituency.

•

[8] *Ibid.*, pp. 4–5.
[9] As Butler notes in discussing staff use, "Most important . . . is the Member's own personality and his own readings of the priorities and responsibilities associated with his position." *Ibid.*, p. 4.

My office is almost 100 percent oriented to doing things that will please constituents, so they will vote for me. And frankly, if you give me twice the staff, they would all be doing the same thing in my district, and in my office.

•

I have eleven people on my staff, and I will agree that the majority of those eleven people are devoted to doing things and listening to problems, and then contacting the departments and working those problems out. I have two people on my staff who never basically contact the public. . . . their job primarily is to analyze legislation, and keep me informed as best as possible with my committee work.

•

Most of the work of my staff is devoted to running the errands, contacting the departments, sending out literature, answering inquiries. A minimum of their time is spent on legislative work. This is dead wrong.

As the last quotation indicates, some members denigrate the value of casework—they do not consider that it is a proper function of a representative. Others take pride in the amount of this type of work which they and their staff can handle. And far from disapproving of these activities, some staff personnel consider the work essential to the representative process (perhaps in part because it is their job—what they were hired to do). One staff aide described such an operation:

As our office is run, there is a certain plateau of campaign operation throughout the two-year period. We hold weekly office hours in our district office, which are announced in regularly scheduled newsletters. . . . Those office hours are anticipated and people are aware, and we have 100 to 150 people per day over a three-day period. Last year he [the congressman] went to [the district] 56 times, at his own expense most of the time, and I went 19 times. What we did primarily for a good Thursday and Friday . . . or Friday and Saturday . . . was to see warm body problems, as we call them. These are people who come [to] us for assistance in any one of the agencies. We established, about four years ago, an appellate structure whereby the [district] staff, which is equally as large as our Washington staff, tries to handle the problem, where the local agency is involved, with the local agency, and if that doesn't work, we get it, to try it on the Washington level of the same agency.

Unquestionably constituency demands would continue even if House members were given a four-year term. Senate staffs are also kept fully occupied with the flood of constituency-related problems.[10] The longer term would presumably have two effects. First, long-term proponents argue that there would be a reduction in the number of constituency-related matters which are picked up at campaign time. Both members and staff agreed that House members tend to get more casework simply because they are forced by biennial elections to go home often:

CONGRESSMAN A: . . . we generate activity by going home all the time.

CONGRESSMAN B: Do your Senators go home every weekend?

CONGRESSMAN A: No. If we were somewhat removed, as the Senators are, we wouldn't generate as much correspondence and questioning. If you go home and go to dinner, by the time you walk from the head table to the rear door, five people will come up to you. "Will you take care of this? It is all written out, and you will understand it tomorrow." You have picked up five matters in that evening.

CONGRESSMAN B: I would hate like the devil not to pick up five matters.

CONGRESSMAN A: So would I. But it generates work.

Staff aides discussed this process from their point of view:

Sometimes it is necessary to be as close to the guy as possible. He is throwing stuff out of a car window and you are picking up the stuff from the sidewalk. At eleven o'clock at night, when he is going home to sleep,

[10] Many, of course, have suggested an "ombudsman" to relieve the members of these tasks. See H. Douglas Price, "The Electoral Arena," in David B. Truman (ed.), *The Congress and America's Future* (Englewood Cliffs, N.J.: Prentice-Hall, 1965), pp. 48–49, and the *Hearings* of the Joint Committee on the Organization of the Congress.

you are going back to the office to unscramble his coffee-spilled notes, and so forth. You all have had that.

•

I spend seven or eight hours, maybe more, on this business [which results from] picking up these things out of the pockets of the congressmen and out of mine. I pick them up and go back at night [to sort them out], sometimes I get up at six o'clock the next morning.

The second effect of eliminating one election, it is argued, would be to reduce the amount of staff time directly devoted to campaign activities. How much time is currently spent on campaign activities? Once again, the answer must be, "It all depends." Significant differences in the campaign activities of top staff aides were apparent in the Brookings round-table discussions. Some aides are campaign managers and are very much preoccupied with that activity during an election year:

I have run my boss's campaign since 1954, as I suppose ———— has. . . . I am the political man in my office, mainly because my boss doesn't particularly care for it. . . . I take care of the machines. We spend about eight weeks in a campaign at which time I go out and run the campaign, not as a campaign manager, but through other people.

•

I guess I am legislative assistant and campaign manager. I work for a member who runs about . . . 60 percent in the final election. . . . Like ———— says, I am the campaign manager. I contract for the billboards and the radio time and the television time and bumper stickers and all that. . . . In the last six months before the final election, then I would say I average out 50 percent [on campaign activities].

These political campaign activities may well include fund-raising:

I can raise as much money as he can raise, because I have more time to do it, and I am not as concerned with answering to the constituency as he is, so my mind is a little freer.

As noted earlier, there is an ethical question involved in using staff in this way. Apparently it depends in part on the constituency as to whether such practices cause difficulty for the member. The following exchange between two House members is illustrative.

CONGRESSMAN A: One of my staff men is going back to the district and instead of doing a job in Washington he is going to be back there working for the next four or five months until the election takes place.

CONGRESSMAN B: Are you going to report his expenses?

CONGRESSMAN A: I am engaging more staff out in the district and not in my congressional office, because it is an election year. If we didn't have that election, that staff would be here performing duties which are more closely identified with congressional legislative work than with campaign activities. . . . I am sure that must be the general attitude in all congressional offices.

CONGRESSMAN B: No, sir.

CONGRESSMAN C: No, indeed.

CONGRESSMAN B: I don't send people back to campaign. That is dangerous business in my district. You can get criticized for it seriously. It can kill you.

Staff aides made similar observations in round-table discussions. As one noted: "I never work on the campaign. [Laughter] How confidential is this meeting? . . . It hasn't happened to me personally but it has happened to senators' aides, other congressmen's aides, if they go back and campaign, they attack them for having their people back in the district."

Even standing committee staff may be drawn into the campaign —writing speeches, providing background material on legislation "that [the members] might have let go up to this time." How much committee staff time is involved and what is the effect? One staff member gave this opinion in the round-table discussion:

It is significant enough, both . . . for the majority and . . . for the minority. I think it substantially impairs the assistance the committees get during the campaign in committee work. . . . In an election year there seems to be so much emphasis on winning that a congressman, although he might be reluctant, utilizes his staff for that purpose, whatever he can get.

Some congressional staff spend very little time on campaign activities. Either the district is safe, or the member prefers to handle campaigning on his own:

> It depends on what kind of constituency you have. . . . If you work for a congressman who is lucky enough . . . to build up 75 percent majorities or 65 percent majorities, then you don't have these same pressures. . . . In our particular office . . . if you would take all of the staff hours in a given year and say how much of these staff hours are being spent on campaigns . . . , I suppose 10 to 15 percent would be all in our office that would be spent along these lines.

●

> From a political standpoint, my member handles everything himself. We have no political organization. We have no full time campaign manager. We have no primary. . . . So I may spend, from the standpoint of what you might call regular political campaigning, perhaps a week or two in the district.

●

> I have not been in our congressional district in the seven years I have been here. . . . If you consider campaigning as what we cannot do under the frank, I do very little campaigning. . . . My boss runs it. He runs his own campaign.

In some cases these staff members whose members come from relatively safe districts may assist candidates in other campaigns—outside their districts—since they are not needed at home.

A strong case can be made that *some* members would gain additional staff time from their not having to campaign every two years. The question then becomes one of how they would use this staff time. More staff time could be allotted to constituency problems or to legislative matters or to both. The proponents of a longer term have in mind that the member would use any additional staff time gained by the four-year term for the legislative function, not for improved or increased constituency service. The staff deficiency at present is in the legislative area. As Charles L. Clapp observes:

> Most House offices probably do not have anyone with important responsibilities in connection with legislation. In fact, the main deficiency in staffing may be the absence of a qualified legislative assistant who can do research for the congressman and help him perform his legislative role more efficiently.[11]

And as Butler indicates in his definition of staff functions, there are a number of legislative activities to occupy staff. Perhaps the most difficult of these is the initiation of ideas—the creativity which results in solutions to public problems. Can it be expected that members will employ additional staff time to assist them in their legislative work? That would depend entirely on the members—on how they define their job. The staff advantages of the long term will not make ineffective legislators effective. Two staff participants in the roundtables explained:

> I think in terms of legislation and serving the district, a good congressman can legislate and serve his district, whether he has a two- or four-year term. A bad and indifferent congressman will not serve his district and not concern himself with legislation, whether he has a two- or four-year term.

> •

> Aren't you really saying . . . if you have a staff that is devoted to errands, that is because the boss wants to be devoted to errands? If you have one or two people that are devoted to legislation, it is because the boss wants it.

This is not to say, of course, that there are no beneficial effects of additional staff for members but that one cannot expect uniformly good results.

[11] Charles L. Clapp, *The Congressman: His Work as He Sees It* (Washington, D.C.: The Brookings Institution, 1963), p. 61. Butler also discusses this problem; *ibid.,* pp. 11–13.

The short-term proponents do not accept the conclusion that constituency-service staff work and legislative staff work can be so neatly distinguished. . . . [M]any of them argue that legislation results from constituency contacts. Thus, when staff personnel are serving the constituency, they are discovering ideas for legislation.

It is very difficult to develop conclusions based on facts, when it comes to the argument over the legislative work of staff. There are no reliable data about the amount of staff time spent on legislative matters—only generalizations about the excessive amount of time spent on constituency service. Neither are there data on the amount of legislation which can be traced to the constituency-service activities of staff. On balance, it does seem that a longer term would provide additional staff time for some House members. Would that staff time be used creatively? Or, can the staff problem be solved in other ways? What constitutes "creative use" of staff? There are presently no objectively derived answers to these questions.

Summary

There are definite policy effects of the two-year term. The evidence indicates that mid-term elections can create real difficulties for the President—particularly a minority party President (e.g., Woodrow Wilson, 1918; and Dwight D. Eisenhower, 1954 and 1958). Most members must take time to campaign frequently and use valuable staff time on campaign activities. And there surely are controversial legislative measures which get postponed because of election-year politics (though analysis of the extent to which Congress willingly goes on record regarding the presidential program does not support this conclusion). But there is much less agreement on the extent to which these are "adverse" effects than is true regarding electoral effects. Thus, there is considerable (though not conclusive) support in this chapter for a longer term for House members *if* one believes that the President should have a friendlier Congress, that members should not campaign as often as they do now, that more staff time should be diverted to other purposes than constituency service, and that all controversial matters should receive attention in election years. If one has other preferences, however, as many congressmen do, then the evidence presented in this chapter will not be very convincing.

Lobbying Activities on the Hill

Paul W. Cherington and Ralph L. Gillen

It is a maxim of political science that the amount of lobbying in a political system will vary directly with the number of points within that system where meaningful decisions are made. We have a national government with separated powers, as well as a vast agglomeration of federal bureaus, agencies, and independent regulatory commissions. Each has a counterpart on the state level; and there are some 90,000 units of local government, many of them also enacting policies with enormous economic and social consequences. All of this in the context of one of the world's most decentralized party systems.

Unlike the British system, in which so many of the nation's policies are controlled by the Government—that is, the Cabinet —the American setting is congenial to lobbying at hundreds of

SOURCE: Paul W. Cherington and Ralph L. Gillen, *The Business Representative in Washington* (Washington, D.C.: The Brookings Institution, 1962), ch. 5, pp. 45–70. Copyright 1962 by The Brookings Institution and reprinted with their permission.

distinct points. Furthermore, the distinctions between the American and British attitudes toward party responsibility help explain the significance of lobbyists in this country. In the United States, the chairman of an important subcommittee in the House of Representatives dealing, for example, with the setting of sugar import quotas is virtually sovereign. His British counterpart would have to answer entirely to the Government for his actions.

There are, then, two separate traditional attitudes toward lobbying in the United States. The first and most pervasive attitude finds the process offensive, smacking of influence peddling, bribery, and arm twisting. It envisions a system geared to the achievements of the general welfare but derailed by those seeking special favors. The lobbyist is a knave and those who succumb to his blandishments are no better.

The second view notes the immense complexity of a system which has made government a part of the life of every person and each business. Government involves each of us, whether we are merely contributing to the Social Security system, checking the daily mail for a message from General Hershey, or, as members of the American Legion, fighting for the continuation of the Subversive Activities Control Board. In a time when many bills are over two hundred pages long and the federal budget is thicker than the New York City telephone directory, many Congressmen find the lobbyist a helpful source of information. Since most members of the House and Senate tend to specialize, the attitude of interest groups toward legislation outside the area of competence of the Congressman is one of his legitimate, indeed vital, concerns. The overwhelming majority of lobbyists are neither cajoling nor threatening. They present information from an admitted point of view, convinced that in the long run this will aid their cause.

Sporadic attempts have been made to regulate lobbying, but they have been unsuccessful. One problem is that the most effective lobbying involves the shaping of public opinion. Huge amounts of money can be spent to convince the nation that a specific bill (or the defeat of a proposal) is in the public interest. Attempts to regulate so-called "grass-roots" lobbying immediately run into First Amendment questions, that is, how would such restrictions affect the rights of free speech and free press.

The lobbyists will be with us as long as big government is so much a part of our lives. They will raise hundreds of voices and some will be louder and more effective than others. If there is a feasible solution to this problem, it has yet to gain acceptance.

In 1957, The Brookings Institution invited nineteen representatives of major firms with offices in Washington to a series of round-table meetings to discuss their responsibilities and operations. These meetings revealed the complexity of the day-to-day functions of the company lobbyist. When schoolteachers descend on a state legislature and demand salary increases, or when the National Rifle Association prevents the enactment of strong gun-control legislation, we all become aware of the influence of lobbying. The merit of the Brookings study is that it places the day-to-day problems and efforts of the lobbyist in a perspective of continuity and a sustained interest in the minutiae of government.

It will perhaps come as a surprise to many readers that the majority of Washington representatives who attended the round-table conferences do not spend the bulk of their time on the Hill dealing with legislative matters. For the popular notion of a Washington representative seems to be that the representative spends every afternoon either on the golf course at Burning Tree carefully losing a match to a couple of congressmen or attending (or giving) a small cocktail party for some influential senators. The mornings would find him in the corridors of the House or Senate Office Buildings or closeted with key committee staff members.

This popular notion is wide of the mark in the light of the evidence of the round-table conferences. Of the nineteen representatives, only one spends the bulk of his time on legislative matters; and his methods of operation are in sharp contrast to those of the popular image.

As was true in the case of marketing and other dealings with the executive branch, no single pattern emerged from the round-table discussions that could be described as "normal" Washington representative behavior on legislative matters. At the early sessions of the round table most of the representatives made a general disclaimer that they ever engage in "lobbying." As the meetings progressed, it developed that virtually all of them deal in some degree with legislative matters, although some of them do so indirectly through trade associations or through company personnel back home. It developed that the disclaimer with respect to "lobbying" went to the point that only a small minority attempt as a regular part of their duties to influence *directly* the passage of specific legislation. It also appeared that, in common with the popular view, or perhaps because of it, the representatives regard "lobbying" as that segment or type of legislative activity that is not quite "nice." It is not surprising, therefore, that most representatives do not wish to be classified as lobbyists.

Two of the representatives at the round table were registered lobbyists and accepted the designation. One of these had been assured by his company's counsel that it was not really necessary for him to be registered but he did so as a precautionary measure. Only one, therefore, did in fact regard himself as essentially a lobbyist. Others acknowledged that to a greater or less degree they work on legislative matters, but the opprobrium attaching to the word is too strong for them to admit to lobbying. As one of the representatives said, "Maybe what is needed here is a different word. I don't think it is the functions that people object to, but the word itself."

Once over the semantics of the representatives' legislative functions, the round table proceeded to explore the substance of those functions, regardless of name. The wide range of the legislative responsibilities of the representatives reflects both differing company interests in national legislation and, more important, significant differences in approach to such problems by company management. Perhaps the following statement comes as close as any to being typical of the companies represented at the conferences:

We have had a variety of attitudes toward how we handle lobbying work. It depends a great deal on who our chief executive officer happens to be and what his opinion is of Washington legislative activity or a particular piece of legislation that we might be interested in.

Usually, however, our work is done through trade associations, and they, of course, work to the point where jointly they come to a conclusion as to what their attitude is going to be. As a member, we support that position to a greater or lesser degree, depending on how our own interests might be affected.

Like many businessmen, the representatives were concerned over the drift of legislative affairs. The companies of several representatives were being, or had been, subjected to extremely unpleasant investigations. They appeared to feel that they were comparatively unsuccessful in getting desired legislation through and that they could block unwanted legislation only with difficulty. Whatever the reason for this feeling, there seemed to be general dissatisfaction among the participating representatives with the current legislative and political climate. At the time of the conferences, the elections of November 1958 had not been held, but there was around the table a keen sense of apprehension as to the possible outcome of those elections, and this forecast of increased Democratic majorities proved to be entirely correct. The attitude of the representatives toward stimulating their companies and their bosses to a greater degree of political activity in a sense heralded the considerable amount of publicity that this subject has subsequently received. This topic will be treated in greater detail at the close of this chapter.

Legislative Functions

One legislative function that the majority of the representatives perform is that of "keeping an ear to the ground" with respect to legislative matters and referring back to their companies what they hear that seems to be of at least indirect interest. Sometimes their ear is kept to the ground at associations and business groups, sometimes on Capitol Hill itself. This listening-post function is performed by virtually all of the representatives at the round table.

Beyond listening and reporting, the other legislative functions performed differ widely. In general it can be said that those representatives who regard themselves as primarily marketing representatives to the government play relatively minor roles in legislative matters. Among the representatives who do take a significant interest in legislative matters beyond the listening and reporting role, there are several means by which they discharge their duties: direct participation; indirect participation through their company; and indirect participation through trade associations, business groups, and professional lobbyists.

LISTENING AND REPORTING

Virtually all of the round-table representatives indicated that at least to some extent they follow legislative matters that have some interest for their companies and report back to management what they hear.

The representative with the broadest program in the legislative area described his listening and reporting function as follows:

We send in a weekly report on bills that we are following; of the 10,000 public bills that were introduced at the first session of the 85th Congress, we were actually following about 1,500.

Most of the other representatives have much less ambitious programs of reporting, covering much narrower ranges of legislation. The majority seem to place a great deal of reliance on their trade associations and on business groups, such as the Chamber of Commerce or the NAM, to alert them to new legislation.

Often we will be alerted to a piece of legislation first by NAM, or the U.S. Chamber. They will catch it first because they can follow these things even more closely than we do; and, along with a copy of the bill, we will report (to the company) the feelings of one or more organizations.

But although a few of the representatives report formally and at regular intervals on legislative matters about which they believe their companies should be advised, the usual reporting pattern is more informal and sporadic. A bill that would affect the transportation of the company's product would be called to the attention of the company's vice-president for traffic, a bill affecting marketing would be called to the attention of the vice-president for sales, etc. Usually the company's general counsel is also advised. The representatives who take a relatively passive part in legislative matters generally make little effort to stir these executives to action. As will be seen, only a minority of the group sees it as part of their responsibility to go beyond reporting and extend their role to active participation in company decisions on what to do about the legislation, if anything. This role may be described as legislative counseling.

LEGISLATIVE COUNSELING

In some companies, the role of the Washington representative goes well beyond that of simple reporting. He is expected to make some suggestions as to whether the company should take a stand on the legislation and to outline a set of tactics to make this stand effective. In some cases the interest of the company in the reported legislation is obvious, and the company executives need no urging to become active. In other instances, especially on broad economic legislation, the representative who is convinced of the desirability of action by his company must do something of a selling job.

There are a lot of bills that particularly relate to our product. We are expected to have a suggestion on them right away. If a bill doesn't directly affect our product, then we may or may not (participate). I have no blueprint that I can follow which will tell me definitely whether or not we will be active.

The decision to become active as a company, or to remain passive, or perhaps to let an association handle the matter appears to be made at the highest level of the company; the chief executive officer has the final say, with the advice of the company's counsel and such functional vice-presidents as may be involved.

One representative, in describing this process, indicated that it was often a difficult task to get a company policy established on a piece of legislation:

The next step is to develop a company policy as to what we are going to do. First of all, are we for or against it? And this is one of the most difficult problems of all—to get the various heads together in the company and decide: "Is this good or bad and, if it is bad, what do we want to do about it?"

The policy having been decided upon, it then comes back to Washington for implementation and there we also need decisions from topside on such questions as: Are we going to testify? Should we lobby in a limited way? . . . Should we use associations?

This representative, whose company is a large one, indicated that he has to rely primarily on executives within the company who would be favorably or adversely affected by the legislation to sell top management on the idea of playing an active role.

Another representative who had more difficulty in getting company decisions on participation had this to say:

Many times you have to project what is going to happen to them (company executives) to get them interested enough to pay attention to what you send.

A third said:

You have to do a selling job on what the effect of legislation is going to be.

The reluctance of companies to adopt a policy on a bill and an active program in support or opposition appeared to stem primarily from the pressure of other business. There was a definite tendency not to participate, especially on legislation that would affect the company only indirectly. Instead, companies preferred to let business organizations represent their interests. Several of the representatives reported that members of their top management believe that "the business of business is business"—making products and distributing and selling them at a profit. This leaves little or no time for getting embroiled in legislative programs, except when the interests of the company are directly and immediately threatened or can be aided. The majority of the representatives tended to deplore this "provincial" point of view, and a few believe that in the past few years their managements have begun to consider their political and legislative interests and responsibilities from a somewhat broader point of view. In at least two instances this wider horizon essentially was thrust upon management by a series of congressional investigations in which the companies fared badly.

But another reason for reluctance on the part of managements to see their companies get involved in an active legislative program is apparently that top executives view such activity as barely respectable. They do not want their representatives to be registered lobbyists. The question was raised why this was so. One member of the conference commented:

The folks back home think it ("lobbyist") is a nasty word, but this doesn't impress me a bit. Granted they have the right to make the decision; but from a practical standpoint, what corporation employee who has registered as a lobbyist has suffered in any way? Do any of you know?

Another said:

I don't think anyone has suffered, but that isn't the whole story. I think a lot of this goes back many years when "lobbyist" was a nasty word. It had a flavor of five percenters and influence peddlers. And yet lobbyists can perform a very worthwhile service to the Congress.

Several of the representatives could be said to engage in "legislative counseling" on a frequent and continuing basis. They regard it as an important part of their over-all responsibilities. The majority of the representatives, however, have limited or occasional opportunities in this field. Whether they do or do not engage in such counseling appears to be related to whether their companies are moving in the direction of some kind of legislative program.

Company Legislative Programs

As previously mentioned, a major problem confronting the Washington representative is to get his company to adopt a policy or program with respect to legislative matters. Very few, if any, of the representatives reported any marked success in getting their companies to think through their policy on substantive economic matters in advance of some specific piece of legislation. Some of the comments were:

The policy on legislation that we are interested in has by and large been developed by my office.

•

For five years I have been trying to get the company to say to me: "This is our legislative program. We want to get from here to here in antitrust, in tax, in all these other fields in which we are interested. These are our long-range objectives."

•

Until now our entire fight has been defensive. We have been fighting brush fires as they have occurred. I contend that we must have a long-range program in, for example, the antitrust field. What changes do we want in the antitrust law?

•

To do this, you have to work with management in the development of its legislative program, among other things.

•

I have made presentations to headquarters in the areas of marketing, antitrust, taxes, and international trade.

•

I, or a member of my staff, will go back and sit down with the staff people with a working paper, saying: "This is where we have been, this is the situation today, this is where we want to go. These are the positions we should take with regard to this legislation." Not one of them has matured today.

•

The decision we have to make is whether there is a basic company interest in a field of legislation, and then we have to develop it from there with the people in the company who should be interested.

This representative had attempted the most ambitious program of any at the round table. One or two others were trying to sell their managements on a broad, far-reaching approach to their legislative objectives in one or another substantive economic area, but relatively little success was reported. Not only are the managements preoccupied with other problems, but there is also apparently serious question as to the wisdom of freezing on legislative objectives in advance of a specific bill. One representative reported that the attitude of his management is: "Why should we?"

In any event, most of the representatives are more than satisfied when they can get their managements to take a position on half a dozen specific issues a year, other than those that directly and substantially affect the company or its industry.

The typical lack of a corporate legislative policy program except in the most extreme cases can perhaps be gathered from the following exchange:

Question: What is your position on foreign trade or foreign aid? Is it the same with every plant?

Answer: I don't think we have taken a position.

Question: So your congressmen do whatever they like. Your congressman in one place might be told, "You ought to vote for this," and another congressman in another district might be advised that he shouldn't.

Answer: I don't think (our people) take any kind of position. It doesn't make too much difference to us.

Question: Do you mean that foreign relations don't make much difference?

Answer: Of course, foreign relations do, yes.

Question: Then how can you say the foreign trade bill is not of much importance to your company? Don't you sell goods overseas?

Answer: Yes, but we have plants all over the world.

Question: Even more reason. At least you ought to have a unified position.

Answer: I agree with you, and it may be that we have, but I haven't seen it.

The need for an explicit company position on legislation and the means for expressing this position to a congressman in a forceful and positive way was emphasized by one of the representatives in the following words:

The congressman may have some interest in, and participate in, fifty or sixty pieces of legislation, and his main interest may be in twenty of them. Let us say that there is an issue that would be important to the corporation, but which is not on the congressman's list. He doesn't know a thing about it. He just goes along with what the state leaders ask him to do.

You go and say to him: "Why did you vote that way on this legislation? We feel strongly about this."

He says: "Nobody ever talked to me about this before. I didn't know you had these feelings about it, and I was afraid if I were for this, that I would lose a lot of votes back home. I didn't think the people back home wanted me to go this way."

We could have given him a lot of help, but I don't think that our machinery and communications are as effective in this field of national policy legislation as they are in (specific legislation). We ought to have a position on all legislation that has any importance.

DIRECT DEALINGS ON THE HILL

The task of the Washington representative in the direct dealings that his company has on the Hill is partly facilitative and partly substantive. He may simply help other members of his company in their dealings, or he may himself appear as a witness or see a member or a staff member of a committee.

Several representatives tend to look at their legislative activities as falling into two categories: those having to do with congressional investigations in which the company is involved, and those having to do with action on pending legislation. Of the two, the investigations are easily the most traumatic experiences for the representative. It is his job to learn of the probability of the investigation. He will probably be consulted by his superiors as to the general climate within which the investigation will be held—the position of the various committee members, opposition groups, and so on. He will probably be called upon to assist in the drafting of the company's testimony, although this will almost certainly be given by one or more top executives and will be prepared back at company headquarters. He will perhaps also be called upon to help prepare the witnesses for their cross-examination. Finally, he will be essentially the host to the company group while it is in Washington. In some cases this job in and of itself is a substantial one since the company may bring to Washington a small army of executives, experts, researchers, and stenographers. This army may be in residence for a week or a month, depending on the schedule of the committee. Throughout the entire investigation the representative must draw on his store of Washington contacts and knowledge to make the investigation as painless as possible for his principals.

But while the congressional investigation puts the representative on his mettle, it is fortunately not a frequent occurrence—at least not for most of the company representatives who were members of the round table. Work on pending legislation consumes more of the time and effort of representatives who are in any way active on the Hill beyond their listening and reporting function.

The round-table participants who indicated that they are active in legislative matters stated that they work on from five to twelve measures a year. One representative said that his company "does something" on as many as fifty bills a year and that he "follows" as many as fifteen hundred a year. But the more usual pattern is for active companies to work on fewer than ten bills a year, and for some of these the major company effort is indirect rather than direct.

The direct action taken varies considerably with the type of legislation, the degree of opposition or support, the interest and position of the sponsoring member of Congress, and the position on the legislation of the executive agencies concerned. In response to a question as to what he does, a representative who took an active part in legislative matters said:

It is hard to pin down precisely. In some cases it may depend on who else is for it or who else is against it. As you know, you are directed sometimes to be for some legislation that is a lead pipe cinch to go through. Then you have a relatively easy job—just registering the fact that you are in favor with one or two people that you think you can talk to.

If something is highly controversial, then an entirely different approach is called for. Sometimes it involves very low-pressure efforts.

Very little direct testimony is given by the representatives, although it is not unheard of. The more usual pattern is for a member of top management to testify, or, if a committee member is from a district where the company has a plant, the local plant head or his representative may be called upon to testify.

I can't think of anyone who has more of an impact on a congressman than a representative of a corporation having a big plant in his area.

Several representatives mentioned that a highly important requisite of management testimony was that the executive be thoroughly prepared. They cited several instances in which top executives of large companies who were poorly prepared had been cut to pieces on the stand—to their considerable discomfort. It was also mentioned that labor witnesses are often better prepared than are business executive witnesses. Thorough preparation and a good witness "personality" are regarded as particularly important in the area of testimony.

But for the most part, the work of the representative in his direct legislative dealings comes outside of the committee room. It is through informal contacts—by telephone and face to face with committee members and committee staff.

My boss and I, not being lobbyists, were limited to those congress-men and senators who represent the states in which our major plants are located around the country; but, as Mr. ———— pointed out, maybe the committee you want to influence doesn't have any of those people on it. So you see a job that needs to be done. You can't do it personally, and therefore you rely on associations, or maybe you can find a friend or a customer who is interested and prod him into action.

Some representatives believe that their informal dealings with members of Congress are of material assistance to the members in giving them the point of view of an important economic unit. In this respect the representative serves as the means through which his company's position can be expressed.

I know them socially, and they don't have any compunction (about talking to the representative). If they want a point of view, they ask for one, and I have no reluctance, when I am visiting with them, to tell them about the problems in my community. I find that many times they need this help. They may have a very strong conviction about some piece of legislation, but are afraid to follow their own conviction because they fear that their constituents will not be sympathetic to the legislation. They need help.

Several of the representatives pointed out that actual legislative technique tends to vary, depending upon whether the company is opposing or supporting a bill.

Almost anyone can be against legislation. That requires a somewhat different technique than being for a bill and trying to get it passed; it is much more difficult, as you realize, to pass a piece of legislation than it is to defeat it. You have more numbers, for one thing, to deal with. It is always easier for a man to be opposed to something new than to be for it. That is human nature.

It should be re-emphasized that no two representatives have the same pattern of direct dealings with the Hill beyond the listening and reporting function. Some stressed their role in congressional in-vestigations of their companies. Others represent companies that have never been investigated. Some work directly on at least a few bills at each session. Others never, or almost never, work directly on legislation at all. Of the nineteen representatives at the conferences, it might be said that only five have regular direct dealings with the Hill on legislative matters.

INDIRECT DEALINGS AT THE GRASS ROOTS

Whether they themselves do or do not have any active dealings with the Hill on legislative matters, the representatives seemed to be unanimous that in many instances company field personnel could be helpful in carrying on a successful corporate legislative program. To this end, several of the representatives indicated that their companies urge plant managers and other local management personnel, wherever they are located, to become acquainted with the local congressmen and senators and then to be able to gain access to them if and when it is necessary. The majority of the representatives said that generally their local plant managers know their local congressional representatives well enough to visit with them socially and to reach them for business reasons as required. A few representatives indicated that this type of local congressional liaison had arisen only in the last few years, and several of the representatives expressed the hope that the liaison could be substantially strengthened in future.

The need for some form of corporate grass-roots support, as envisioned by the representatives, stemmed in part from the grass-roots organizations of other interests. Labor unions, the postal carriers' organization, and the Grange were mentioned specifically. As was brought out earlier in this chapter, grass-roots congressional liaison in some cases was established because an opposition group had this type of liaison. But in most cases the need for local support for the corporation was a reflection not so much of the fact that opposing groups had interests conflicting with those of the corporation as it was of a desire to maintain a voice at least as loud as do these organizations, one that would not be drowned out in the hubbub of Washington. Thus the general thrust of the move to gain legislative access through the grass roots appears to stem essentially from a desire to maintain a channel of communication between congressmen and senators and their constituencies.

We do not call upon local plant people or local officials of our company around the countryside to bring their influence to bear in this area of legislation. This is a shortcoming that my boss and I are trying to change. For example, a congressman on a committee handling a piece of legislation in which we are interested may be from City X, where we have a plant. Well, City X *is* our company since its very existence hinges on us. He may be a staunch Democrat, but he still knows there are a lot of voters in that plant. Wouldn't it be a lot more effective if the general superintendent of that plant contacted him rather than for us to contact him in Washington?

When you consider that we operate in maybe twenty states, that suggests a potential of forty senators and at least twenty or thirty congressmen. If you had that many friends on Capitol Hill, you would have a pretty good entree for any problem.

In a majority of the companies represented at the round table, the local plant managements know their congressional delegations. But although this avenue of communication is available, it seems in many cases not to be used, except sporadically and in case of a real threat to the corporation. Even when the local plant managements visit with their congressmen in Washington and in the districts, there is evidence that they make little attempt to put across the company's point of view on a legislative program. This somewhat surprising fact stems apparently from the lack of a position on anything except the most threatening legislation. It also reflects the indicated reluctance of the companies, by and large, to have their employees engage in anything approaching lobbying.

Another representative expressed the somewhat different position of his company in these terms:

Somebody in our company—in top management at headquarters, in the Washington office, or in plant management—knows all the congressmen and senators from the areas where we have plants. But our company has asked the question, "How would congressmen and senators regard our (legislative) activities?"

We believe that you could become something of a pest to congressmen and senators if you went in with a position on every issue that came up.

We prefer to have it understood by our congressmen and senators that, when we go to them, it is on an important matter that is related to our activity in their state or district. We must rely on the NAM and the Chamber of Commerce to have a position on most bills that come up. It would be a mistake to take too many positions because very quickly the congressmen would say: "Who do these fellows think they are? Are they trying to run me?"

And if you touch their pride in that way, I don't care how close you are, you are going to hurt yourself in the long run.

To the extent that a grass-roots approach was used, the following statements are almost textbook rules of thumb in the area of legislative access. One participant said:

I have found, and I am sure all of you have too, that those people who are influential have, for one reason or another, been able to put themselves in a position back at the grass-roots level of being able either to help or to hurt the congressman or the senator. That is a rather cold-blooded way of putting it, but after all there is a balance of power. Sometimes it means votes, sometimes it means helping him financially, and sometimes it is a combination of both. Labor does this kind of thing, and they have more manpower than we have; but industry certainly could play a bigger part, and top management should encourage local plant managers to take a more active part in legislative matters that particularly affect its industry.

A second comment was:

I think American industry has a great story to tell, and we have found that most congressmen are willing to listen. But they want you to be with them at times other than when you are asking them to do some special favor for you. You can't be in there asking them for a favor and then forget them until the next time you want a favor.

And again:

We have found, in trying from time to time to make our influence felt with certain legislators, that almost every congressman and senator has certain people in his district that he listens to. They may be the strong financial backers or the publisher of a paper whom he has faith in and listens to. Usually there is a key to everyone. Our local people, our local officers and plant managers in the area, should be alert to the problems here in Washington; and they could find out, if they didn't already know, whom a particular congressman listened to. Maybe they wouldn't even do the personal contacting, but they might talk to Joe Smith at the Rotary Club, who in turn had the ear of the congressman. There is no set pattern to this thing, and you can't say it will work the same way in each district. It varies from district to district.

I do think all of us have a responsibility to try to get our companies interested in doing something of this kind.

There was some discussion at the conferences as to whether the use of the grass-roots approach could "backfire" on the company, especially whether top management would be charged with dictating to their local plant personnel on political matters. This question was answered as follows:

The intention there is not to try to force a view on the people in the plants, but (1) to give them at least an enlightened presentation and make sure that their congressman knows that this is the company's appraisal of the situation—that these are the facts, and (2) in the light of this, to ask what he intends to do. The congressman then knows that you are going to be watching what he does, and this has a very salutary effect.

A small minority of the representatives have some reservations about the effectiveness of the grass-roots approach, especially when it is used on a hotly-contested issue.

I would like to ask this question though. Suppose the plant manager makes known to the congressman how the company feels about a certain bill. Suppose that the congressman says, "Well, so what? The company feels that way about it. Does the plant management, do the laborers, do the families of these people, do the voters feel the same way? How many votes has the company got in my area?"

The answer usually is, it doesn't have any.

One representative, whose company had drastically changed its policy in the direction of a much more active legislative program a year or so before the round-table conferences were held, described the change and the new grass-roots program at some length:

. . . it was a very nasty fight that we lost, and it resulted in a bill that tended to regulate our industry.

We had never had a Washington office as such until 1951, and for a number of years earlier some of us had been trying to preach the gospel of an aggressive program. Finally, when we did get into trouble, the change took place. They reactivated the office on a different basis, and we have launched a rather far-reaching, long-term program. I would like to emphasize the words "long-term" because I, for one, and I am sure my principals, don't expect much to happen overnight—I don't think much *could* happen overnight.

We looked at our principal competition and at the labor unions to see what they do in the political field and what they do with the grass-roots program. Then we looked at what the XYZ group had. They had one of the most beautiful grass-roots programs that I have ever seen.

Then we began an about-face. First of all, the lines of communication with the principals in headquarters were opened considerably.

Second, we started a grass-roots program, which involves all of the locations that we have throughout the United States—all of our plants, our district sales offices, our public relations offices. The program here is obviously, as a first step, to acquaint our people in the field with their congressmen and also to acquaint them with the legislative problems that are of direct interest to, and have an effect on, the company.

I spent all last fall—after Congress adjourned and until Christmas —out in the field, introducing our people to their congressmen. I think the best story that came out of the whole effort was the first meeting I had in City Y. I outlined the program (to our people), describing what we wanted them to do. I got all through, and the district manager said: "Well, I can't do that. I have a memo from the company that says I cannot talk with anybody who holds an elective office."

It was dated 1946, and he was still operating under it. This was the old approach to things, but it was still his Bible and the motivating force within the field organization. It didn't take long to solve that problem.

Few of the companies represented at the round table have experienced as dramatic a shift in policy and approach toward the grass roots as that just described. In addition, only one other representative participates as actively as does this one in grass-roots planning and tactics. But although their participation is less dramatic and less direct, several of the representatives take part to a limited degree in operating the grass-roots apparatus that their companies have developed for legislative purposes.

DEALING THROUGH ASSOCIATIONS AND SPECIALISTS

Note has already been taken of the fact that for most legislation many companies prefer to work through business or trade associations or through legislative specialists retained for the purpose of setting forth the company's position on a particular bill.

The use of a specialist was described by one of the representatives in the following way:

> We may be of the opinion that the congressional committee examining a piece of contemplated legislation does not have a clear view of all the facts in the case and that it would be to our interest to be sure that they did have. Then we hire these people (specialists) to visit with our people at headquarters and get facts applying to the case to submit as expert testimony.
>
> Usually when the man we hire goes up, he has two or three technical people, if it is a technical subject, that he can consult with.

There are, of course, a considerable number of law and public relations firms in Washington that specialize in legislative representation. One of these firms was described as follows by a representative whose company uses this type of specialist quite extensively:

> The particular firm we use is a well-established Washington firm with a history of considerable success in this field. They are qualified,

they are very vocal, they are very careful, they have a very fine reputation for being effective people, good witnesses, supported by good factual preparation. I am sure there are other companies represented around the table here that hire counsel of this type that are experienced in presenting testimony.

Several other representatives mentioned that their companies use such specialists in the handling of legislation before committees to which they feel they do not have particularly good direct access. They are used also if the company feels that an association could not fully represent its position or where no association is involved. A question was raised as to the relative value of informed legislative work done by a specialist in Washington vs. a real grass-roots operation. One member commented:

I think that depends on the problem. I don't believe you can set down any rule of thumb as to which is more effective. On some of these things—where you have a relatively narrow issue, where he can be briefed, and where he can make a forceful presentation along one line—a specialist may be much better.

On the other hand, if you have a relatively wide-open situation—and I would refer to this———hearing as being such a situation—it seems to me that a top executive of the company, with a row of experts behind him, can do a much better job.

But the more usual channel of outside representation on legislation is apparently through associations and business groups. All of the companies represented at the round table use this channel, at least to some extent, and some use it to the virtual exclusion of any direct approach.

In the development of association policy on a piece of legislation, the Washington representative tends to play essentially a facilitative role. He is in frequent contact with the legislative staff of his specialized trade association and with those of more general business associations. On a particular issue, he is apt to call in experts from company headquarters to help in formulating and presenting the association's position. When this is done, the role of the representative is much the same as it is in the case of direct representation on the Hill. He reports on prospective association legislative activity; he may help the company to develop a position, but he is usually not the company's formal spokesman at association meetings.

The eagerness of companies to be represented before the legislature by an association is due to the same reasons that they prefer such representation before the executive branch: they gain strength from an *industry* rather than merely a *company* position. But legislative representation by associations appears to stem in part also from a desire for anonymity by management and their suspicion that active legislative programs are faintly unrespectable.

A trade association visitor invited to one of the round-table meetings, who has extensive dealings with legislative matters, made the following observation in response to a statement by one of the representatives that his company rarely, if ever, gets involved directly:

That is the trouble. That is the real trouble. The individual companies look to the trade associations, and they (the associations) are no better than the individual members themselves.

This trade association man went on to say that when his group had a legislative problem that it was handling for the industry, it did its best to get the individual company members to participate actively in presenting the matter to the Congress. It also tried to get help from other trade groups but usually found that these groups had other problems of their own.

One disadvantage of being represented through an association or a business group is the difficulty of developing a hard-hitting and effective program in the association. This apparently applies with particular force to general business groups developing a position on broad economic legislation. Some of these difficulties were described, as they referred to labor legislation, by one representative as follows:

I think one of the problems that confronts management and industry in general in connection with this labor problem is that we are not united. The unions are all united on all legislation.

Industry—any one industry or any one management organization—is in competition with another management organization. We try to tie it up through the U.S. Chamber or through the NAM.

If you ever attended meetings of the NAM, you would see how disorganized they are because no two industrial people will agree. They can't seem to come to an agreement; and until management can come to an agreement around a table in the Chamber of Commerce or the NAM, with a unified approach to a problem, you are never going to get strength equivalent to that of the unions. It can't be done.

One industry management does not trust another one because they are always in competition in their normal activities, whereas the unions are hardly ever in competition with each other. . . .

One of the representatives stressed the need to use local or state associations, as well as those in Washington, in the handling of legislative matters. This was, in effect, adding a grass-roots dimension to the legislative approach through associations.

My view is that the trade associations can do a fine job, but they can do it only up to a certain point. They can gather information, disseminate it, and act as guiding hands in these legislative fights. In our industry we have found that local trade associations, or the regional general business associations, are more effective than those that deal just with industry problems; it is much more effective to work through them than to depend on the NAM or the Chamber of Commerce, to which most of our large companies belong.

Although several of the representatives, like those above, expressed doubts about the effectiveness of associations in legislative matters, it nonetheless appeared that it is through this channel that the companies represented carry on the great bulk of their legislative dealings. In such situations, it is the task of the representative to keep in touch with the association's position and its tactics, to assist it where he can, but more important, to serve as a link between the association and his company.

The Political Posture of the Company

At an early round-table meeting, one of the representatives passed around a four-page pamphlet, put out by the U.S. Chamber of Commerce, which had as its centerpiece an aerial view of downtown Washington. Identified in the picture were the national headquarters of numerous labor unions. The text of the pamphlet pointed out that labor had seen fit to locate their union headquarters at the seat of the national government so as to get the full benefit of the political advantages which such proximity gave them. The implication was clear that here was business's political opposition and that businessmen would be well advised to equip themselves with a countervailing political program.

Especially at the round-table meetings devoted to legislative matters, the discussion moved back and forth between the legislative activities of the companies and their over-all political posture. It was clear that the two are intimately related. And while certain of the representatives see the political posture of their companies primarily in terms of a conflict between labor and management, others recognize some broader political aspects. But however they look at the political scene, all of the representatives were concerned with what they regard as the increasing political potency of the unions. In this regard, they had some hard things to say about the political abilities of business and businessmen:

As someone said, management is naive politically; they don't know how to operate. A labor union knows how to operate. It is organized and determined and works twenty-four hours a day.

Or again, these comments:

They (the unions) have ability in a grass-roots system.

•

They have pretty good liaison with the committee staffs too. They know what is coming.

•

They instigate a lot of your investigations; they know the trends; they are ready to back up the statements that they have already given to the committee staff.

•

. . . industry has different objectives. For instance, we are interested in sales, we are interested in production, but labor unions are interested in people; they are interested in social reform. You can't beat that.

•

. . . one reason why corporate management doesn't take a bigger interest is because most of them have never been in politics and are not trained in dealing with public officials. They are all interested in how fast they are going up the ladder, and they don't want to take too much time dealing with politics when a potential rival may be working full time increasing sales or something of that sort. There is just as much politics in big corporations as there is in the federal government and sometimes even more. While you would think that, because of that fact, they would have a better understanding of the political problems, they apparently do not, and they all shy away from it.

Another aspect of the same phenomenon was expressed as follows:

The statement was made a little while ago that our management people at home are pretty naive about all of this. I think you could even go so far as to say that management is showing a surprising degree of isolationism, while the labor groups are showing a degree of not only national but international statesmanlike interest.

Now, (the unions) may be fumbling for the best way to handle themselves, but they aren't fumbling from the standpoint of the amount of effort they are putting in.

There are a lot of things that have no constituencies and are straight national and global policy matters. You will find labor has a very strong, well thought out view of them. Not only that, they have the courage of their convictions, and they have all kinds of communications media to get these convictions out to the public.

Therefore, when you get into some kind of a public issue that affects us as a nation among nations, you find that labor is the first one to take a position. This should not be the case. We have the capacity to bring out a much greater performance on the part of business-statesmen than labor has with labor-statesmen.

There was, to be sure, some evidence cited to the effect that businessmen were beginning to become increasingly aware of the political power of the unions.

I think that industry is starting to awaken to the fact that labor has moved into Washington and that they have no compunction about pressing pretty hard on things that they think ought to be done by Congress; and they make sure that the representatives in Congress from their districts know what their views are.

Certainly management has as much at stake as the individual workmen who are members of unions, and in many cases it has much more.

In almost the same breath, however, several representatives expressed the view that labor is acquiring increasing political power all the time. For example:

Congressional district by congressional district, it (labor's political power) has grown tremendously. Whereas at one time the public officials of the cities and the states were probably the most influential group, I would say that now the labor group is the most influential.

Or again:

There is no question but that the labor lobby in Washington is the most powerful one in town.

Another pointed out:

The congressman's office is always open to a labor man. They know what they are doing, and they are as effective as can be. It is not open to the businessman to the same degree. He doesn't represent as many votes.

Again:

One congressman told a group that for every representative of business who called on him there were fifty representatives of labor, and that unless business did something about this, it couldn't ever hope to accomplish anything legislatively in Washington to offset this terrific lobby that labor has.

In common with most businessmen, the representatives were puzzled by just what could be done about the situation. The build-up of large business groups as a countervailing power against the unions or other groups with differing views seems at best to be only a partial solution primarily because of the diversity of business interests and the difficulties of reconciling them.

There is so much diversity in industry's interests. You take the (large business group) weekly or monthly publication, its legislative summary. You read that over and it really has very little of any value because they never take a position one way or the other. They will report fully on Social Security, or some nice, safe topic; but if you want anything out of them as an authoritative statement, you will have to go down to their files and pick it up because they are not going to put anything in writing that will disturb any portion of their membership.

Others believe that at least a part of the answer lies in a closer relationship between businessmen and elected officials:

Some of the more thoughtful people in the business community make it their business to get acquainted with their congressmen and talk to them about the problems that affect their particular community from the standpoint of the plants in that area. This makes it possible for the fellow to do a job in Congress. There is a considerable amount of work done by people who see that their representative in Congress has all of the help and all of the advice that he can get from the plant and from company management to guide him in what he is trying to do.

But several of the representatives are of the opinion that a broad corporate political action program is necessary in both the policy and the tactical areas. In this regard, their views tie back into those set forth earlier in the chapter on legislative programs. These representatives, and they include some whose companies have started in this direction and also those whose companies have not, tend to view the problem more broadly than a tactical struggle with labor. They believe that the program would have to be all-encompassing, ranging from management help in selecting nominees and candidates and helping the "good ones" get elected down through and including working closely with any elected official regardless of party affiliation. The question was asked whether this means that businessmen should get some kind of political action program of their own. One representative replied:

We had better, or we are going to be sunk. As I see it, that is what will happen.

Another said:

We have been talking specifics tonight about what the Washington representative does in this area, and that is a very narrow part of this whole thing.

As I envision it, first, we have got to get our local people interested in our national legislative problems, but, even more basic than that, we have to help people to run. Good candidates are what we need, and you will not find one businessman out of a million willing to tackle that problem.

Another representative indicated that he regards a corporate political program in two distinct segments—what happened before the election and what happens afterwards. He believes that prior to the election corporate management should see that good people were nominated and that good nominees are supported and elected. In this phase of the program the Washington representative would play no part, nor would the corporation as such. The second phase would involve relations with the congressman or senator who was elected. Here the Washington representative would play an active role, acting as a link between the corporation and the elected official in Washington. Local plant management would in turn keep in touch with the official and his friends back in the state or district.

The question was raised whether it is realistic to think that the two segments can be kept separate. In reply, the advocate said:

If we should elect an unsympathetic official in a district where we have a plant, we could try to work with him down here and encourage our plant people to work with him at the grass-roots level. Even if he is pure anti-business and has no interest for us, sometimes we might make a dent. If not, sooner or later I would get together with our general superintendent and say: "Can't we defeat this guy the next time around?" But I would not go out and organize anything. That would be up to the people at the local level.

It should be added that the program just described was essentially prospective and had not been implemented, except on a sporadic and *ad hoc* basis.

By and large, the political posture of the companies represented appeared to be neutral or nonexistent. It was the view of at least several of the representatives that a more positive posture would help their legislative efforts.

Summary

Much of the discussion in the foregoing chapter applies exclusively to those Washington representatives who play an active part in the legislative process. Of the representatives at the conferences, those who play a continuously active role were a small minority. About half of the group can be said to have had some role in legislative matters. A few have had virtually nothing to do with legislation beyond reporting to their managements on legislative affairs of concern to the company.

Beyond the reporting function, several of the representatives are called upon periodically to consult with their managements concerning company policy and tactics on legislation. In this regard, they reported that it is often hard to get their managements to take a position on a pending bill and virtually impossible to get them to take a general policy stand on a broad economic issue in advance of specific legislation.

There are essentially three ways in which a company's legislative interests can be furthered: by direct dealings on the Hill, by the use of grass-roots pressure, or through specialists and associations. A good deal of the work of the representatives in these three areas is facilitative in that they make arrangements for others in the company to carry out the legislative function, but a number of representatives are heavily engaged in direct activity in one or more of these areas.

Inevitably the question of the company's political posture, as it affects the company's legislative fortunes, was discussed. Most of the plans for improving this posture appeared to be in prospect rather than already accomplished, although one or two companies had taken active steps in this direction.

In sum, the legislative role of the representative appears to be substantially smaller than might be supposed. It shows promise of expanding in the future.

Focus on the Combatants: The Appropriations Committees

Jeffrey L. Pressman

Every civics class heading for the Capitol is reminded that seeing the House and Senate in action is quite likely to be a disenchanting experience. The real work of Congress is done in committees, is the old maxim, and so the visitor is somewhat mollified when he sits in the gallery and sees a handful of Senators paying little attention to a mumbled speech. If, then, the average citizen is reconciled to the system, it is because he has presumably learned to distinguish the real from the visible.

He presumes, for example, that each committee is a microcosm of the parent body; that is, the Ways and Means Committee of the House or the Judiciary Committee of the Senate is a representative miniature. The members of every committee become specialists in the very technical business they confront and they respond, in the main, as members of a political party. The full House and Senate are therefore inclined to accept the recom-

SOURCE: Jeffrey L. Pressman, *House v. Senate* (New Haven: Yale University Press, 1966), ch. 3, pp. 28–52. Reprinted by permission.

141

mendations of their committees because they are representative
of the parent bodies.

As Professor Pressman points out in the selection that follows,
these assumptions are only partially valid for the Appropriations
Committees of the House and Senate. We can safely add that
they are equally dubious as an analysis of the entire committee
system.

Ernest S. Griffith once noted that the seniority system "is a
spirit pervading the total behavior of Congress," and that the
committees must be seen in that context. In both Houses and in
both parties, the methods of selecting committee members give
preference to seniority, and the chairman of each committee is of
course the senior member of the majority party. He in turn selects the chairmen of the subcommittees. This is a power of increasing significance for, as the work of the Congress becomes
more and more specialized, the influence of some 240 subcommittee chairmen expands proportionately.

The House and Senate have their norms and these too influence
the committee system. Members always seek and often win the
committee assignment that will allow them to serve the special
problems of their constituencies. It is therefore not surprising
that, in the 90th Congress, six of the seven members of the Subcommittee on Tobacco of the House Agriculture Committee were
from southern tobacco states or that a Senator from South Dakota headed the Subcommittee on Indian Affairs of the Interior
and Insular Affairs Committee. Interest groups have ways of
making their wishes known, and it is quite common to find that
members who have articulated the views of labor or management receive committee assignments where they will be dealing
with proposals that matter a great deal to those groups.

Beyond this is the congressional doctrine of "responsibility."
The most important committees in both Houses are always be-
sieged by many conflicting forces. If those who make the committee assignments share a notion of the "responsible" legislator,
that is, a profound concern for the customs and traditions of the
institution itself, it is not surprising that the powerful committees
reflect that view of responsibility. Historically this has meant
that in the House and Senate, southern Democrats and rural Re-

publicans have exercised far more power than their numbers would justify.

Yet the attacks on the committee system have had to be oblique, for there is no likelihood that seniority itself can ever lose its primacy, if only because no alternative poses fewer problems. In 1966, the Joint Committee on the Organization of Congress sought to reduce the prerogatives of committee chairmen by recommending a "Committee Bill of Rights." It urged that all committees have regular meeting times, for example, and that rules be adopted "to insure that the members always have an opportunity to work their will." The Committee's many recommendations have not been adopted, although there is some evidence that the publicity which attended the hearings has made many chairmen more responsive to their colleagues.

For the foreseeable future, then, any analysis of the committee system must recognize that each committee is itself a social system which has, within congressional norms, its own folkways and habits, often the reflection of the unique personalities who guide it at a given moment.

What . . . are some of the agencies of Congress which most directly affect the economy, which do or can serve to give a measure of coherence to economic legislation? Here selection is imperative; every committee of Congress has some impact. But the appropriations committees surely must be considered. Not only does the level of federal spending have direct and enormous influence on economic activity, but every piece of legislation which requires spending, and nearly every activity which wants to go on, must pass in review before these committees.[1]

The power and importance of the House and Senate Appropriations Committees have long been recognized by students of politics. And

[1] Ralph K. Huitt, "Congressional Organization and Operations in the Field of Money and Credit," in Commission on Money and Credit, *Fiscal and Debt Management Policies* (Englewood Cliffs, N.J.: Prentice-Hall, 1964), pp. 403–4.

there is evidence that observers outside the social science community are becoming aware of the crucial nature of the appropriations committees' work. A recent article in *Science* magazine notes that, as football experts watch the movement of the line to understand each play, so many students of Congress focus their sights on the appropriations committees.[2] For in these committees, vital decisions are being made: where to spend money, where to cut back, which government programs to encourage, and which programs to strangle by cutting off funds. It is to the House and Senate Appropriations Committees themselves that this study now turns. Without an understanding of the structure and operations of each committee, it is impossible to see the causes for conflict between the two and the preconditions necessary for reform in the budgetary process.

Surprising as it may seem to those who have confronted the entrenched and powerful appropriations committees, the clear-cut jurisdiction of these committees over all spending bills is just 45 years old. The Ways and Means Committee was established by the House of Representatives in 1802 with responsibility for both taxing and spending. A separate Committee on Public Expenditure was created twelve years later, but five additional committees were set up in 1816 to review the decisions of this committee.

In 1865 the House formed an Appropriations Committee; in 1867 the Senate followed suit. Once again, however, jurisdiction was split up over the years among several additional committees. Actually, unity of control came as a response to the Budgeting and Accounting Act of 1921. The legislature was now faced by a genuine budget from the executive side. As a reaction, Congress placed all spending power in its appropriations committees.[3]

[2] *Science,* 143 (February 7, 1964), 548–51.
[3] Huitt, p. 429.

The House Appropriations Committee: Wielder of Power

Throughout the years, as has been noted, custom has conceded to the House the right to initiate appropriations bills. The House committee is larger than that of the Senate and its members can devote more time to appropriations business than can the senators (who must serve on other committees as well). Therefore, the House committee has historically played a larger role in the appropriations process. Furthermore, the chief obstacles to budgetary reform are to be found in the House Appropriations Committee. For these reasons, the discussion of the House committee will be more detailed than that of its counterpart in the upper house.

In a study of the House Appropriations Committee,[4] Richard F. Fenno gives evidence which clearly points up the fact of House committee power. Of 443 separate case histories of bureau appropriations examined, the House accepted Committee recommendations in 387 (or 87.4 per cent) of them. In 159 (33.6 per cent) of the cases studied, the House committee's original recommendations on money amounts were enacted into law without change.[5]

The words of a former congressman offer further testimony to the power of the Appropriations Committee. Discussing the "ways to get things done in Congress," the late Representative Clem Miller remarked:

To tackle the Appropriations Committee on the Floor of the House is a major decision, frequently the most important decision a Member will make that term of Congress. Here is the choice. If he is silent, perhaps the Senate will restore the item to the bill. If he speaks up and is beaten, he will *never* get it back. And the chances of winning are

---

[4] Richard F. Fenno, Jr., "The House Appropriations Committee as a Political System: The Problem of Integration," *American Political Science Review,* 56 (1962), 310–24.
[5] *Ibid.,* p. 323.

better than five hundred to one against. These odds mean silence to most congressmen.[6]

Nowhere is the committee's power more acutely felt or more bitterly resented than in the field of foreign policy. In theory, the Appropriations Committee merely determines whether all of the dollars requested to carry out what Congress has authorized are really needed. The money committees do not, it is supposed, alter the substance of policies. Of course, practice does not always conform to theory. Holbert N. Carroll, viewing the Appropriations Committee warily, pointed out that

the Committee on Appropriations . . . is the most powerful agency of control over the course of policies and their administration in the House of Representatives. Almost all important foreign policies require money for support, so in deciding what funds shall be allowed, and in sundry other ways . . . the committee wields great influence over the substance of policies. Since the decisions of this committee follow in the wake of formal policy decisions, its word is the last word, so far as the House is concerned, respecting these policies.[7]

The committee exercises its power in a variety of ways. First and foremost among its weapons is the power to cut off an agency's funds. In three areas studied by Professor Carroll (occupation funds 1946–51, foreign aid 1947–56, and State Department budgets 1945–56), the executive branch submitted estimates totaling $54.8 billion. The committee reported 88.7 per cent of the funds requested by the executive, and the voice of the committee was the voice of the House. In thirty out of thirty-five major appropriations, the House simply endorsed the committee's bill.[8] To demonstrate its disagreement with the large-scale European recovery program, the

[6] Clem Miller, *Member of the House: Letters of a Congressman* (New York: Charles Scribner's Sons, 1962), pp. 39–40.
[7] Holbert N. Carroll, *The House of Representatives and Foreign Affairs* (Pittsburgh: University of Pittsburgh Press, 1958), pp. 141–42.
[8] *Ibid.,* p. 154.

committee slashed more than one billion dollars from the Marshall Plan's funds.

. . . [C]ommittee *reports* can often be used to exercise control over executive branch activities. Another weapon of the committee is the insertion of limitations and legislative provisions in bills themselves. The rules of the House forbid legislation in appropriations bills, but limitations which specify that no part or only a fraction of an appropriation may be used for a certain purpose are quite in order. And sometimes limitations of a distinctly legislative nature slip through the House unchallenged. Thus, in providing funds for aid in occupied countries in 1947, the committee added a provision that the countries to receive aid "shall be expected to provide, in agreements to be signed by their governments . . . for reimbursement to the United States for such aid." [9] The Appropriations Committee had initiated a major policy innovation.

"STANDING LIKE A STONE WALL": THE SELF-INTEGRATION OF THE HOUSE COMMITTEE

In an exchange with a member of the House Appropriations Committee, Representative Clarence Brown remarked bitterly that when an amendment is offered

to reduce an appropriations item, the Appropriations Committee stands like a stone wall most of the time, saying "no, you mustn't touch this." That is one of the things that has brought complaint against your committee, sir, and you know it . . .[10]

The committee does seem to stand like a "stone wall." In contrast to the House Committee on Education and Labor, where lack of internal unity resulted in the inability of that committee to propose a successful federal aid to education bill during the Eisenhower and

[9] *Ibid.*, p. 168.
[10] Aaron Wildavsky, *The Politics of the Budgetary Process* (Boston: Little, Brown, 1964), p. 50.

Kennedy Administrations,[11] the House Appropriations Committee is remarkably well integrated. Fenno suggests that this tight integration is in large measure responsible for the power and legislative success of the committee.[12] In 1964 most of the congressmen and staff members interviewed mentioned the high degree of cohesion found in the House committee and some attempted to give explanations for it. Because committee integration may have some effect on House strength in conference situations and House committee resistance to reform, it is necessary to examine the reasons for it.

The need for integration in a given social system arises from the differentiation among its constituent elements. A committee must make these diverse parts work together in support of one another. Committee integration may be defined as the "degree to which there is a working together or a meshing together or mutual support among its roles and its subgroups." [13] A concomitant of tight integration is the existence of control mechanisms—rewards and penalties—which are capable of maintaining conformity to the norms.

Fenno's work on the House Appropriations Committee focuses on the period 1947–61. His analysis includes a listing of characteristics of the committee which help explain the integration of its parts and a description of the control mechanisms that preserve integration. The present study makes use of Fenno's outline and general explanation of committee integration, but the analysis here is based on interviews carried out in the Spring and Summer of 1964. Therefore, relevant examples and illustrations will be drawn from the more recent interview material. At certain points, Professor Fenno's analysis will be qualified.

First of all, Fenno sees integration aided by a well-articulated and deeply rooted consensus on committee goals and tasks. The

[11] Richard F. Fenno, Jr., "The House of Representatives and Federal Aid to Education," in R. L. Peabody and N. W. Polsby, eds., *New Perspectives on the House of Representatives* (Chicago: Rand McNally, 1963), p. 352.

[12] Fenno, "House Appropriations Committee," p. 323.

[13] *Ibid.*, p. 310.

committee's view is rooted in the traditional preeminence of the House in appropriations affairs. Moving from this, the committee sees itself as the most important unit in the appropriations process. For the committee, its most important task is guarding the Federal Treasury—usually by cutting down budget estimates. And the House committee does indeed cut estimates. For the purposes of a larger study, Fenno examined the case histories of appropriations for 37 executive bureaus over a twelve-year period: 1947–59. Of 443 separate bureau estimates, the committee reduced 77.2 per cent of them.

However, one must be careful of the generalization that House Appropriations Committee members are budget-cutters. The *Science* article referred to above also commended Representative John E. Fogarty (D., R.I.) for his knowledge of scientific and medical affairs. As chairman of the subcommittee on Labor-Health, Education and Welfare Appropriations, Fogarty has consistently championed the cause of the National Institutes of Health. Further, there are members who identify with an agency or with specific programs. "To me, forestry has become a religion," once remarked Representative Walter Horan. And Daniel Flood has kept a protective eye on Defense Department appropriations.[14] Thus, Fenno's identification of committee consensus may be qualified to say that budget-cutting is not the *only* role which motivates Appropriations Committee members. The exceptions must be taken into account.

Integration in the Appropriations Committee is also facilitated by the subject matter with which the group deals. Writing in 1943, Macmahon spoke of the traditional "appropriations type: hard-working, hard-bitten." [15] Fenno observes that a money decision does not seem to be a vital policy decision; thus members are relatively free of "liberal" and "conservative" roles inside the committee. "The Appropriations Committee is the banker for the federal

[14] Wildavsky, p. 48.
[15] Arthur W. Macmahon, "Congressional Oversight of Administration: The Power of the Purse," *Political Science Quarterly* (March, 1943 and June, 1943), 161–190, 380–414.

government," drawled one southern House committee member in 1964. "Appropriations bills are more or less dull. They all concern dollars and cents. Nothing we do is really earthshaking—we finance programs, that's all." Integration appears to be further facilitated by the fact that a man recruited for the Appropriations Committee is first informally certified as a "responsible legislator"—defined as "one whose ability, attitudes and relationships with his colleagues serve to enhance the prestige and importance of the House of Representatives." [16] Such a man has a basic respect for the legislative process and appreciates its informal rules. This quality is the most important criterion for assignment to the three top House committees—Rules, Ways and Means, and Appropriations. In the interviews, the friendly southern congressman commented that "the members of this committee are picked carefully—believe me." Only "responsible legislators"—those who are willing to compromise and who are dedicated to the ways of the House of Representatives—need apply.

Another factor in the committee's integration is the attractiveness of the Appropriations Committee for its members. This strong attraction increases the influence which the committee and its norms exercise on all members, for "it increases the susceptibility of the newcomer to Committee socialization and of the veteran to Committee sanctions applicable against deviant behavior." [17]

Note has already been made of the "appropriations type"—hardworking and industrious. Consider the following statistics:

The House was in session 141 days during the first session of the Eighty-sixth Congress. In that period the Defense Subcommittee of the Appropriations Committee . . . met sixty-five days, nearly always in both morning and afternoon sessions. For nearly three and one-half months the subcommittee met almost daily on the dual meeting basis. In 1963, the Defense Subcommittee met seventy-two and one-half

---

[16] Nicholas A. Masters, "Committee Assignments," in Robert L. Peabody and Nelson W. Polsby, eds., *New Perspectives on the House of Representatives* (Chicago: Rand McNally, 1963), p. 46.

[17] Fenno, "House Appropriations Committee," p. 314.

working days, excluding the period required for marking up the Defense Appropriations bill.[18]

Committee members revel in their role of hard-working legislators. "We try to build up respect for each other on the committee. We think we're the hardest working committee in Congress," remarked a conservative member of the committee. Observed a young liberal: "I may sound critical, but a lot of hard work is done by those subcommittees. . . . They are very conscientious. No glory, no public hearings . . . this is a working committee."

These characteristics of the House Appropriations Committee—consensus, careful recruitment, nature of the work, and committee attractiveness—help to explain the integration of the committee. But how is integration maintained? By what mechanisms are decisions made?

The committee carries on its day-to-day work in subcommittees, each of which is given jurisdiction over a number of related governmental units. The chairman of the full committee sets the number and jurisdiction of subcommittees and appoints their chairmen and majority party members, while the ranking minority member decides which minority members shall be included. Each subcommittee holds hearings on its agencies' budgets, writes the full committee's report on those agencies' appropriations, and handles the debate on the floor. And each subcommittee, within its jurisdiction, is proudly independent. "Subcommittee chairmen are kings unto themselves," said one Republican member. Another member—this one a Democrat—remarked that:

Rather than a committee, this is a collection of thirteen principalities. When we have a meeting of the full committee, it is perfunctory and almost pro forma. Although the issues are thoroughly gone into in subcommittee, you have no chance to do so in full committee. Try to get reports in advance, and you find that it is a tightly guarded secret.

In order to make this policy of subcommittee autonomy work,

[18] Charles L. Clapp, *The Congressman: His Work as He Sees It* (Garden City, N.Y.: Doubleday Anchor Books, 1963), p. 267.

a norm of specialization exists. Each member is expected to play the role of specialist in the activities of one subcommittee. Conflict among subcommittees is reduced by the deference traditionally accorded to the recommendation of the subcommittee which has "the facts." An older committee member observed: "There is great specialization. And look at the *esprit de corps* in the committee." Furthermore, integration is facilitated by the norm of subcommittee unity, a willingness to support the recommendations of one's own subcommittee. (If the norm of reciprocity—the custom which requires that each subcommittee respect the work done within every other specialized unit—functions to minimize conflict in the full committee, then the norm of unity minimizes conflict within the subcommittee.) There is a tradition against minority reports in both the subcommittee and the full committee. During the period 1947–57, for example, only 9 out of a possible 141 were written. Also, there is a tradition of nonpartisanship within both the subcommittees and full committee. The committee has a nonpartisan staff; requests for studies by the committee's investigating staff must be made by the chairman and ranking member of the full committee and also the chairman and ranking member of the subcommittee involved. With party conflict minimized, integration is facilitated. "Partisan loyalty fades almost entirely," remarks one member, while another adds: "There are no Republican–Democrat battles. This is just not natural—it's phenomenal!" [19]

One source of internal cohesion and integration is the effective control mechanism of socialization and sanction. Members must learn to see the world around them with some degree of similarity. A liberal member of the committee has remarked:

[19] One exception to the rule of nonpartisanship was the creation, in the 88th Congress, of the "Bow" task force of House Republican members of the committee. This group worked in cooperation with the minority leadership to cut the President's budget. One member, Rep. Pillion, observed "For the first time in my memory, the Republican members of the Appropriations Subcommittees worked as a team with specific appropriation reduction targets." See John S. Saloma, III, *The Responsible Use of Power: A Critical Analysis of the Congressional Budget Process* (Washington; American Enterprise Institute, 1964), p. 33.

The Appropriations Committee develops a strange sort of breed. As soon as you get on the committee, somehow you become more responsible as a member of Congress. You find you have to justify expenditures and you cannot pass over any situation very lightly. As a result you become more conservative.[20]

Socialization is carried out by a system of rewards and punishments. For the member who serves his apprenticeship on the committee, who follows the norms of subcommittee autonomy and unity, who does not express dissent on the floor, there are rewards—perhaps prominent floor roles, perhaps a subcommittee chairmanship.

For those who insist on breaking committee norms, there are punishments. One liberal had this to say:

We had an appropriation in the Interior bill for the Kennedy Cultural Center. In subcommittee, we discussed it—and I thought the subcommittee decided on a ridiculous location. I said so on the floor. Boy, was my subcommittee chairman furious! He gave me a tremendous tongue-lashing.

Another remarked:

On the foreign aid appropriation, I filed dissenting remarks with the clerk. They didn't print them, and the chairman told me that they wouldn't print minority opinions unless they came from that subcommittee's members. Believe me, I've gotten into a lot of trouble for sounding off like this . . .

In the 1964 interviews, liberals who criticized committee procedures justified their willingness to "go along" by declaring their great admiration for the work of their subcommittee chairmen. Thus, a northern Democrat remarked: "Al Thomas and Rooney are good men . . . really great. And Rooney knows what he's doing . . . he talks tough but his bark is worse than his bite." Thus, we may add another factor promoting committee integration: respect for the men who lead the subcommittees.

[20] Clapp, p. 243.

Fenno's emphasis on subcommittee unity and autonomy may be modified slightly. At times, intervention by the chairman of the full committee may be necessary to curb actions by a subcommittee chairman which block party programs deemed vital. Thus, in the summer of 1964, Representative George H. Mahon, new chairman of the Appropriations Committee, lobbied actively to save President Johnson's foreign aid bill from its annual emasculation at the hands of Representative Otto Passman (D., La.) in the Foreign Operations subcommittee.

Still, Fenno's analysis seems to be borne out by interview material collected in 1964. The consensus, attractiveness, and recruitment policies of the Committee on Appropriations make it susceptible to tight integration. Decisions are made in specialized subcommittees, and dissent and partisanship are discouraged. Each subcommittee respects the work of the others, and all members stand together on the floor. Finally, to encourage compliance with the set of norms (i.e., informal but authoritative rules for behavior), a system of rewards and punishments is maintained. All of this keeps the House Appropriations Committee functioning as a cohesive and well-integrated unit. Potentially divisive subgroups —conservatives and liberals, rural and urban men, Republicans and Democrats—are brought together and mesh to form a well-functioning whole. Conflict is minimized, and work can go on effectively.

THE ROLE OF THE CHAIRMAN

Although the appropriations subcommittees are fairly autonomous, the power of the chairman of the full committee cannot be denied. For it is he who selects the subcommittee chairmen and the majority members of each subcommittee. Clarence Cannon, who was chairman of the committee until the spring of 1964, put his unique stamp on the House Appropriations Committee.

In 1956 he [Cannon] reorganized the subcommittees, in the course of which he deprived Rep. Vaughn Gary, who was perhaps not sufficiently staunch in his opposition to the foreign aid program, of the chairman-

ship of the relevant subcommittee . . . [and he] would have gone further, were he not restrained by the protests of his senior colleagues on
the Committee . . . In 1962 he reached into the budget for the Defense Department . . . plucked out the Civil Defense program . . .
and assigned it to a subcommittee whose chairman opposed the program. In 1963 five liberal new members were placed on the Committee
by the leadership, replacing, on the average, more conservative men.
Cannon gave all but one of the new members low-level jobs in the
Committee's equivalent of Siberia: subcommittees on the District of
Columbia, on the legislative budget, and for a man from New York
City, the subcommittee on agriculture. Meanwhile, senior members
whose views were more congenial sat on three or four important subcommittees simultaneously.[21]

One senior member of the committee remarked that "Cannon is
always there when they mark up a bill." Another explained that
"the subcommittee chairmen are really kings of their own castles.
But Cannon can be the swing vote on markups. On Public Works,
Cannon can work with Republicans to kill a bill."

However, Clarence Cannon did not prove immortal—perhaps
surprising some Washington observers. On May 12, 1964, he died
of a heart ailment at the age of 85. The new chairman was George
H. Mahon of Texas, and the *New York Times* was quick to evaluate the newcomer:

Administration leaders do not expect any sudden change in the 50-
member committee's conservative budget-cutting proclivities. Mr. Mahon, like his predecessor, is a conservative and an outspoken advocate
of economy in government. However, it is generally accepted that the
63-year-old Texan will be much easier to work with than was the
crusty, 85-year-old Mr. Cannon.[22]

Prophetically, the *Times* went on to note that "a possible by-
product of the shift in chairmen is a gradual decline in the power

[21] Nelson W. Polsby, *Congress and the Presidency* (Englewood Cliffs, N.J.:
Prentice-Hall, 1964), pp. 91–92.
[22] *New York Times,* May 13, 1964.

of Otto E. Passman, Chairman of the Foreign Operations sub-committee." We have already indicated that this decline did indeed occur. Instead of supporting Mr. Passman, as Mr. Cannon had done, the new chairman used persuasion effectively to turn Pass-man's subcommittee against its chairman by a vote of 7–5 and thus to save the Administration's foreign aid package in 1964. The following winter, at the start of Congress, Chairman Mahon stacked Passman's subcommittee overwhelmingly against him. When the subcommittee voted a generous foreign aid bill in the summer of 1965 (trimmed by only $75 million), Representative Passman de-cided to serve as floor manager of the bill anyway. What followed was one of the weirdest performances in Congressional history:

For 52 minutes, while he presented his own bill to the House, Passman savagely attacked it and all "the imaginary accomplishments of the foreign aid program." And then, after fulsome apologies, Passman turned around and started fighting for the bill. "I represent the major-ity of the committee and not necessarily my personal views," he said. "It will be my responsibility to defend it to the fullest extent of my ability." When Republicans moved to cut $285 million out of it, Pass-man declared: "I hope the motion will be voted down." [23]

As the *Times* had predicted, the area of foreign affairs was the scene of the major change in appropriations policy under the new chairman.

Interviews with two high-ranking House staff members confirmed the *Times'* assessment. One remarked: "There have been no sig-nificant changes in the House committee since Mahon took over. He is not the type to rush in. There will be differences, like in foreign aid. But basically Mr. Mahon is at least as conservative as Mr. Cannon." The other offered much the same analysis:

Mahon is averse to using brutal power. But he realizes that he is the chairman. He is just as vigorous as Cannon, although less spectacular. And Mahon is as conservative as Cannon, but not as obvious about it. I mean he doesn't adopt a meat-axe approach and cut willy-nilly.

[23] *Time,* September 17, 1965, p. 38.

Neither the temperament of the chairman nor the solidarity of the committee encourages sweeping changes. And, although Mr. Mahon is not as pugnacious as his predecessor, much hostile feeling still exists between the House and Senate Appropriations Committees. For, as we have shown, hostility between the committees runs deeper than the personalities of committee chairmen. (Although Mr. Mahon might not be as active a catalyst of conflict as was Mr. Cannon, it must be remembered that a change in Senate committee leadership might make that group *more* pugnacious. So there are still possibilities of open battle in the future; . . . legislators in 1965 worried about House-Senate feuds and tried to devise ways to deal with them.)

Still, Mr. Mahon *has* made a change in an appropriations subcommittee, and that change may be instructive for those who would make further alterations in the appropriations process. In 1964, the chairman was able to go over the head of a subcommittee chairman to ensure passage of a party measure in an election year. At that time, the power of the party over its members was strong enough to win out over subcommittee loyalties. Further, the change was incremental and came in stages. In 1964 Chairman Mahon used persuasion to change the votes of subcommittee members. In 1965 the chairman of the full committee reshuffled the membership of the Foreign Operations subcommittee to make it more "reasonable." These were incremental changes, particularly applicable to a budgetary process in which sweeping alterations are shunned.

THE HOUSE STAFF: PROFESSIONALISM AND NONPARTISANSHIP

"We have a good appropriations staff. Nobody's political friend is on the staff. These people come from G[eneral] A[ccounting] O[ffice]—and Mr. Cannon keeps it that way—no political influence. You know, a competent staff is the right arm of this committee." With these words, a liberal member of the House committee paid tribute to a committee staff which is well known for its hard work and lack of partisanship.

Each subcommittee has access to professional staff assistance. Unlike most congressional committees, the Committee on Appropriations has had a history of employing professional help that reaches back into the 1920's; today, the committee conducts a modest training program to develop the competence of both senior and junior staff members.[24] The majority and minority each employs a small political staff which is separated from the bulk of the professional staff.

In numbers, the staff of the Appropriations Committee appears large. In the late 1950s the size of the staff averaged about sixty to seventy-five employees. (The numbers have remained remarkably stable from 1951 to the present day.) But these figures include stenographic and clerical help; only twenty could really be classified as professionals. There were also two or three investigators employed by the committee and a large number of special investigators borrowed from the executive branch for temporary duties (for the second half of 1955 there were thirty-four such investigators on the committee's staff).

Whether or not the staff of this committee is adequate to its task has been argued back and forth for years. In the interviews, Appropriations Committee members from both houses expressed the view that a larger professional staff was needed. However, the controversy over staff size is not a main concern of this study. Suffice it to say that the staff of the House Appropriations Committee, by its nonpartisan nature, reduces the chances for partisan conflict on the committee. Furthermore, the competence and unusual *esprit de corps* of the staff deepens the attraction which the committee has for its members and thus aids cohesion and integration.

The Senate Committee

Although the Senate Appropriations Committee is only half as large as its counterpart in the House (twenty-seven as opposed to fifty members, to be exact), and although it waits for the House

[24] Carroll, p. 148.

to act before submitting its own report, the Senate committee is not weak. It is composed of senior and powerful men, like Richard B. Russell of Georgia, Warren G. Magnuson of Washington, Mike Mansfield of Montana, and Thomas H. Kuchel of California. In the second session of the 84th Congress, the Appropriations Committee contained nine chairmen or ranking minority members of other committees, the Democratic floor leader and whip, the Republican floor leader, whip, and Policy Committee chairman.[25] Of the twenty-three men who made up the committee in the 85th Congress, five had been in the Senate more than twenty years, another twelve for ten years or more, and only one less than six years. Most had been members of the House of Representatives, seven for more than ten years. Among them, they represented 303 years of service in the Senate and 428 years in Congress.[26]

The Senate committee is obviously an attractive one. A senior member said: "The Appropriations Committee in any legislative body is at the top . . . In the Appropriations Committee, you find the greatest education in government. The spread of jurisdiction is tremendous." One indication of difference in committee attractiveness is the movement of senators from one committee to another. Because any change in committee assignment involves a loss of committee seniority, a change usually indicates that a senator prefers the new committee to the old. In an attempt to measure the relative attractiveness of committees, Donald R. Matthews constructed a chart showing the net effects of all changes in Senate committee assignments during the 1947–57 period (see Table 1). The extreme right-hand column shows the net gain or loss of each committee.

Based on this measure, the Committee on Appropriations is second only to Foreign Relations in attractiveness. One reason seems obvious: a member of the Appropriations Committee is in a position to "do more for his constituency" in terms of federal

[25] Donald R. Matthews, *U.S. Senators and Their World* (New York: Vintage Books, 1960), p. 151.
[26] Thomas E. Barth and Sandra Jo LeGath, *The Appropriations Process in the Senate* (unpublished M.A. thesis, University of Wisconsin, 1960).

160

TABLE 1

NET GAIN OR LOSS OF COMMITTEE MEMBERSHIP THROUGH
CHANGE OF ASSIGNMENT, 80TH THROUGH 84TH CONGRESSES

Committee	Foreign Relations	Appropriations	Finance	Armed Services	Agriculture	Judiciary	Commerce	Banking & Currency	Interior	Public Works	Labor	Government Operations	Rules	Post Office	D.C.	NET TOTALS
1. Foreign Relations		+2	+2	+1	+2	+1	+1	+1	+1	+3	+2	+3	+1	+1	+1	+16
2. Appropriations	−2		+1	+2	+1	+1	+1	+2	+2	+3	+1	+1	+1	+3	+2	+15
3. Finance	−2	−1		+1	+1		0	+1	+2	+2	+1	+3	+2	+1	+1	+10
4. Armed Services	−1	−2	−1		+1	−1	+1		+2	+1	+2	+2	+1	+1	+3	+4
5. Agriculture	−2	−1	−1	+1			+1	+1		+1	0	+2	+1	+1	+1	+7
6. Judiciary	−1	−1		−1			0	0	0	+1	+1	+1	+2	+4	+1	+8
7. Interstate & Foreign Commerce	−1	−1	0	+1	−1	−1		0	+2	+2	+2	+2	+3	0	−1	+1
8. Banking & Currency	−1		0		−1	−2	0		0	+1	+1	+1	+1	+1	+2	−2
9. Interior	−1	−1	−2			−2	0	0		−1		+2	+1	+4	−1	−5
10. Public Works	−1	−3	−2	−1		−1	−2	−1	−1		+1	+1	+1	+1	+3	−6
11. Labor & Public Welfare	−2	−1	−1		−1	−1	−2	−2	−1	−1		+2	+1	+4	+2	−11
12. Government Operations		−3	−2			−2	−2	−3	−1	−1	−2			+1	−1	−9
13. Rules	−1	−1	−1	−3	−3	−1	−2	0		−4	+1	−1		+1	+3	−19
14. Post Office	−1	−3	−1	−1	−1	−1	−4	+1	−1	−2		−3	−3		+4	−17
15. District of Columbia	−1	−1	−2	−1	−3	−1	−1	+1	−1	−2	+1	−1	−4	−1		−17

SOURCE: Matthews, *U.S. Senators and Their World*, p. 149.

projects. (Thus, Senator Mansfield's position on the Appropriations Committee was crucial in the decision by that body to appropriate money for the minting of silver dollars in the summer of 1964. This decision, of course, helped the silver interests in Montana tremendously.) Furthermore, it is felt that an Appropriations Committee member can exert more influence in his dealings "downtown"—with the executive branch.

In 1962 the senators demanded that they be given the opportunity to initiate one half of all appropriations measures. But the interviews showed that members of the upper house felt pressed for time under their present duties. One senior member of the Senate committee observed: "In the Senate, too many people have to serve on too many committees. There is a *tremendous* amount of time required, and I have so much to do. I may have two to six meetings in the morning. Shall I divide my time among these? Or shall I specialize?" With Appropriations Committee members serving on (and sometimes chairing) other major committees, how could they possibly hope to initiate and hold lengthy hearings on half the appropriations bills? The senior committee member had this answer: "The Senate could initiate appropriations, but it would have to make time for this. We would have to spread ourselves less thin. In fact, I would say that the Appropriations Committee members should have no other committees." Perhaps the Senate's demand in 1962 for the right to initiate appropriations can best be understood as a demand to be used for bargaining purposes. At any rate, the Senate committee at the present time does perform a distinctive function in the appropriations process, and it is to that function that the study must now turn.

THE COURT OF APPEALS

The Senate has acted as an appeals agency. The House trims, and the agencies run with their tear-jerking story to the Senate. "We got 98% and we're going to wail and groan about the 2% that the House cut out." They pick out the things in which the Senate is the most interested.

Thus a House committee staff member described the appellate function of the Senate Appropriations Committee. A Senate subcommittee chairman remarked: "It would be an effort in futility for the Senate to go into each detail. In practice, the Senate has emphasized the effort to reverse House decisions."

In 12 of 21 appropriations for fiscal 1958 involving over half the total appropriations, the Senate restored all or part of the cuts made by the House.[27] Further evidence of the Senate's appellate function is found in the testimony of committee members. In 1957 Senator Magnuson, chairman of the Independent Offices subcommittee, sent letters to all heads of affected agencies asking if the "public interest" required any changes in the House appropriations bill and whether they wanted to arrange a hearing. Also, when Secretary of Commerce Weeks assumed that the Senate subcommittee would consider his whole budget (and not just the six items appealed by the department), Senator Holland set him straight: "The lack of appeal would indicate . . . that you think the other cuts except in the six items which you want to mention will not be so harmful as to require your making an appeal . . . In other words, we are not going to appeal for you." [28]

As Huitt notes, however, there is one potent restraint on appeals (and this restraint operates more effectively on service agencies like the Library of Congress than on agencies with strong and well-organized clienteles). That is the prospect of facing the members of the House committee the year after a successful appeal has been carried off. The next time, the cut might be deeper. For the House might count on the Senate's exercising its power to rescue the agency again.

In foreign affairs, the Senate committee exercises an appellate function in regard to both funds and policy directives. Of thirty-five major appropriations in the three foreign policy areas studied by Carroll, the Senate raised the House-approved sums in twenty-four. The executive branch submitted estimates calling for almost $55 billion for the thirty-five major appropriations. For all three areas combined, the Senate committee approved sums 6.7 per cent

[27] Huitt, p. 434.
[28] *Ibid.*

higher than House-endorsed sums. Senate sums were 14.9 per cent higher in the area of occupation, 6 per cent higher in foreign aid, and 3.5 per cent higher for the State Department.[29]

It is interesting to note that the appellate behavior of the Senate committee extends to substantive matters as well. Phrases are sometimes inserted in the reports of the Senate committee to permit administrators to evade some of the detailed and bothersome instructions contained in House reports. In 1948, when the House committee slashed Marshall Plan funds by about one-fourth, the Senate committee restored a substantial portion of the money cut out by the House and also removed or changed legislative decisions sponsored by the House committee which diverged from decisions approved in the authorizing committees.

A WORD ON THE STAFF

The Senate committee has enjoyed marked continuity of staff, as has its counterpart in the lower chamber. Thomas P. Cleaves was clerk from 1873 to 1910 and Kenneth F. Rea served from 1910 to 1939. Everard H. Smith, the present clerk, took that position in 1939.[30] As in the House, Senate staff spirit runs high. One assistant remarked: "We get our talent from the executive branch, and they had better be trained in accounting. The pay is lower on the Hill, but it's worth it to be with this committee." Professional talent—including accountants and lawyers—is hired from the executive branch. Senate staffers are proud to be with the committee and recall with avid interest the House–Senate battle of 1962. House members are seen as "irresponsible," and special condemnation was reserved for Representative Otto Passman, the once terrifying villain of Foreign Operations conferences. In all, the competent Senate staff serves for its committee a function similar to that provided by the House staff for its superior body. The staff adds a further element of attractiveness and cohesion to the Senate Appropriations Committee. Of course, the staff's attitude toward the House does

[29] Carroll, p. 291.
[30] Macmahon, p. 184.

not encourage peaceful relations between the committees, and Senate staffers were quick to say—without regret—that House–Senate conflict could easily break out again.

Thus, at the center of the appropriations process, there are two proud and powerful committees. Filled by some of the most prominent men in Congress, the two groups have very different roles. The House committee, viewing itself as the voice of economy, seeks to cut excess "fat" from the appropriations requests of various agencies. On the other hand, the Senate committee, perceiving itself as the defender of responsibility and continuity in government, serves as a court of appeals for agencies whose budget requests have been cut by the House. The House (in most cases) slashes funds; the Senate (in most cases) restores either part or all of the House cuts. Somehow, these forces must meet; the matter must be resolved. A figure must be settled upon which will be acceptable to both sides. Thus the matter moves to conference committee.

Congressmen and Their Constituencies

Lewis A. Froman, Jr.

There are many times in the study of government when the explanation of a complex problem can be relatively simple. Why a member of the House of Representatives or the Senate votes as he does may often bewilder the student of public affairs, particularly when that student's public policy goals are treated callously by the Congress. However irrational those votes may appear, they are thoughtful, deliberate judgments made by elected representatives who are invariably convinced that they are acting on behalf of their constituents. Putting the matter even more directly, the politician who seeks martyrdom is rare indeed; the fundamental notion of survival insures that he will seek to accommodate those interests and voters who sustain his career. He may make the occasional decision that the wishes of his constituents can be thwarted, but in the overwhelming majority of instances he will, as the saying goes, "vote the district."

This is not nearly as restricting as it appears. Many of the

SOURCE: Lewis A. Froman, Jr., *Congressmen and Their Constituencies* (Chicago: Rand McNally, 1963), chs. 6 and 7, pp. 69–97 (tables have been renumbered). Reprinted by permission.

165

same voters who worry about inflation are also concerned that our defense budget be adequate and that postal services be maintained. Every voter will have an attachment to a variety of policy goals, each of which can be approached in many different ways. Indeed, the politician knows that separate problems will generate separate coalitions of interest; a civil rights question will activate one set of groups, while the prospect of import quotas on certain raw materials will set off a totally different cluster of constituents. Only infrequently does a politician confront a constituency where a majority of the voters are so concerned about the specific details of a particular bill that he has no mobility at all. More typically, the politician will understand the effective forces within his district and will seek to respond to them.

He will of course feel other pressures at the same time. The leader of his party may be seeking his support on a measure that will displease powerful constituents. The President may promise future favors that will assist his district if he will go along on a particular proposal. His colleagues on a committee may also prevail on his loyalties to that group. Thus, in each instance, his judgment on how to represent his district may require a balancing of sensitive factors; yet the focus of that judgment will be precise.

If the Congressman is constantly weighing questions on the basis of how the answers will affect his constituents, there are two major questions that remain as we seek to explain the process more fully. First, we must concede that the politician is perceiving his constituency. Although aware of the forces that make their presence felt, he must also understand the attitudes of those who may be affected by an issue but have made no overt appeals. The problem this poses for representative government is quite easy, however painful it may be for the representative. We note that the politician who guesses wrong frequently enough is out of a job. Having misrepresented the wishes of his constituents, his fate is in accord with the rules of the game.

The second question is more formidable. What happens when several interests or groups within a constituency are so well organized that they can exercise a far greater influence on public policy than their numbers would justify? The politician is far more sensitive to organized effective power than to large dissatisfied groups that are not strong enough to translate their attitudes into votes. The dilemma is an easy one for the politician to resolve; he will respond to realities. The student of government, however, will note with some resignation that the failure of many voters to make their presence known all too frequently means that those who have the greatest need for the benefits of government may not be capable of extracting them.

The fate of gun control legislation in 1968 is illustrative. Shortly after the assassination of Senator Robert F. Kennedy, President Johnson proposed legislation that would have required the licensing of guns and the registration of gun-owners. Despite the fact that the polls showed that some 80 percent of the nation was in favor of strong legislation, the proposals failed.

Among those who opposed the President's demands were such usually reliable supporters of administration domestic policies as the majority leader in the Senate, Mike Mansfield of Montana, the majority floor leader in the House, Carl Albert of Oklahoma, and Democratic Senators Philip A. Hart of Michigan, Frank Church of Idaho, George McGovern of South Dakota, and Eugene J. McCarthy of Minnesota. While these men may have represented constituencies that were generally in favor of the Johnson proposals, they confronted in their daily work, not the placid majority who were supporting the proposals, but the vocal, highly organized minority who saw licensing and registration only as preludes to confiscation. The politician may be responsive to his constituency, but the voting on this issue was a response to the intensity of attitudes, not their dimensions.

In the selection reprinted here, Professor Lewis A. Froman, Jr., points out why members of the Senate are more likely to support welfare state measures than are members of the House and how the different economic characteristics of House districts affect roll-call votes. Students who wish to test Professor Froman's conclusions might well study Senate and House roll-call votes on the many programs that are related to the nation's urban crisis.

Why the Senate Is More Liberal
Than the House

This [section] will deal with how the manner in which members of representative institutions are elected and the kinds of constituencies of which the institutions are composed can affect the type of public policy which is likely to flow from those institutions. That is, electoral systems, as well as many other procedural rules, are not neutral in their impact on the course of public policy. For example, we are all familiar with the argument that the manner in which the President is elected has a significant influence on the public policies preferred by presidential candidates as opposed to the average congressional candidate of the same party. The operation of the Electoral College under the unit rule specifies that the winner of a plurality of votes in the state wins all of the electoral votes in that state. Because this unit rule in the Electoral College gives candidates an added bonus if they can win the states with large electoral votes, presidential candidates tend to overrepresent large, urban, two-party states, and minority groups within these states.[1] This is an example of how the procedural rules can affect the content of public policy proposals.

Similarly, we can expect that the fact that senators represent whole states while congressmen represent relatively smaller, more homogeneous districts within states might have some impact on the type of legislation preferred by the average member in each institution. We [now] explore how this difference in type of constituency represented affects the public policies which are likely to be produced within the Senate and House of Representatives.

---

[1] See Robert A. Dahl, *A Preface to Democratic Theory* (Chicago: University of Chicago Press, 1956), chaps. iv and v; and Lewis A. Froman, Jr., *People and Politics: An Analysis of the American Political System* (Englewood Cliffs, N.J.: Prentice-Hall, 1962), chap. vi.

THE INTENT AND CONSEQUENCES OF A BICAMERAL LEGISLATURE

Commentators on American political history find that the compromise to establish a bicameral national legislature was expected to have the following consequences: (1) the upper house, or Senate, was to be more representative of the well-to-do, propertied classes in the United States, and (2) the lower house, or House of Representatives, was to be more attuned to "mass" pressure, especially from the debtor, unpropertied, lower classes. This, of course, was in addition to the large vs. small state controversy which a bicameral legislature also helped to solve. Hence, state legislatures, not "the people," were to elect senators; only the members of the House were to be elected by the general population. The anticipated consequences of a bicameral legislature elected in this fashion were that the House would be a more liberal body, the Senate more conservative.

Recent observations of Congress seem to belie these expectations. Although systematic studies are lacking, current commentators point out that the Senate is more liberal than the House. Undoubtedly, changes in the method of electing senators, as well as the expansion of the franchise, have had a great deal of influence on the policy preferences of senators as well as congressmen. But these changes merely help to explain why there should be no differences between the Senate and the House. Both are now popularly elected by a system which allows for universal suffrage. Why should the Senate be more liberal than the House?

Two problems will occupy us in the next three sections: first, to answer the question, is the Senate more liberal than the House?, and second, to provide an explanation for the answer.

IS THE SENATE MORE LIBERAL THAN THE HOUSE?

Evidence for the proposition that the Senate is more liberal than the House will be presented in two different ways. First, we shall inspect all of the bills submitted to Congress by President Kennedy during the First Session of the Eighty-seventh Congress to ascertain how they fared in the hands of each house of Congress. Second, we shall examine, in much closer detail, ten of President Kennedy's most important requests for legislation to see how each bill was amended by the Senate and the House. The first measure will provide a comparison between the Senate and the House in the treatment of President Kennedy's legislative program. By making two assumptions, we can infer something about the liberalism of the Senate as compared with the House. The second measure will allow us to apply a much more rigorous definition of liberalism to a comparatively few bills in each house. The first measure has the advantage of breadth, the second of detail.

The *Congressional Quarterly Almanac* lists 355 pieces of legislation submitted by President Kennedy in the First Session of the Eighty-seventh Congress.[2] These 355 pieces of legislation represent specific requests for legislative action by President Kennedy. Of these 355, 10 were treaties. Since the House does not act on treaties, these have been excluded from the analysis. Also, of the twenty-nine tax bills (which must originate in the House), twenty-three did not get beyond the hearing stage in the House of Representatives. These twenty-three are not counted since there is no basis of comparison with what the Senate might have done. Our list of 355, then, is pared to 322.

These 322 bills were then scored by the *Congressional Quarterly Almanac* as to whether they were treated favorably or unfavorably by the committees in each house of Congress and, if they reached this stage, on the floor of each house of Congress. When modifications of the original requests occurred, the *Congressional Quarterly* evaluated the outcome to determine whether it was closer to approval or disapproval of the President's request. On the basis of the scores provided in the *Congressional Quarterly Almanac,* the number of favorable and unfavorable committee and floor actions in the House were totaled and compared with the number of favorable and unfavorable committee and floor actions in the Senate for

[2] (Washington, D.C.: Congressional Quarterly, Inc.), XVII, 91–103.

the 322 pieces of legislation submitted by President Kennedy. It can be inferred that the body which has the greatest number of favorable actions, and least number of unfavorable actions, is more liberal. This inference follows from the tenable assumptions that President Kennedy is a liberal, and that the program which he submits to Congress is a liberal program. Table 1 presents the data on favorable and unfavorable committee and floor actions in the House and Senate.

The data in Table 1 support the hypothesis, as measured, that the Senate is more liberal than the House. In committees and on the floor, the Senate acted favorably on a larger percentage of Kennedy's proposals, and unfavorably on a smaller percentage, than did the House. In the committee stage, the Senate acted favorably on 207 (64.3 per cent) and unfavorably on 44 (13.6 per cent) pieces of legislation compared with 192 (59.6 per cent) and 56 (17.4 per cent) respectively in the House. Similarly, in floor action, the Senate acted favorably on 185 (57.4 per cent) and unfavorably on 51 (15.8 per cent) of Kennedy's proposals, the House, 166 (51.5 per cent) and 66 (20.5 per cent), respectively. Although the differences are not large, each of the comparisons supports the hypothesis. Additional confirmation is also supplied by the slight differences found in the "No Action" columns. If Kennedy's program is considered liberal, and if the Senate is more liberal than the House, we would expect greater inaction on the part of the House as compared with the Senate. Table 1 confirms this additional deduction.

The above data, however, must be used cautiously. Certainly it is not being argued here that all of the 322 pieces of legislation submitted by President Kennedy may be classified on a liberal-conservative continuum. Hence, findings such as the above which may entail such an implication should be supplemented by other data. To provide a more detailed treatment of the question of which house of Congress is more liberal, ten Kennedy proposals were chosen for closer examination.

The *Congressional Quarterly Almanac* lists twenty-five bills as

TABLE 1

FAVORABLE AND UNFAVORABLE COMMITTEE AND FLOOR ACTIONS IN THE HOUSE AND SENATE ON 322 PIECES OF LEGISLATION SUBMITTED BY PRESIDENT KENNEDY, 87TH CONGRESS, 1ST SESSION*

	Actions on Kennedy Legislation					
House of Congress	Committee			Floor		
	Favorable	Unfavorable	No Action	Favorable	Unfavorable	No Action
	N %	N %	N %	N %	N %	N %
House	192 (59.6)	56 (17.4)	74 (23.0)	166 (51.5)	66 (20.5)	90 (28.0)
Senate	207 (64.3)	44 (13.6)	71 (22.1)	185 (57.4)	51 (15.8)	86 (26.8)

* Data from the *Congressional Quarterly Almanac* (Washington, D.C.: Congressional Quarterly, Inc., 1951), Vol. XVII.

being the most important of Kennedy's requests facing the First Session of the Eighty-seventh Congress.[3] Eight of these twenty-five had to do with foreign affairs and reorganization of the executive branch and were eliminated. Of the remaining seventeen having to do with domestic welfare programs, ten were randomly sampled for more detailed analysis.

These ten proposals constitute the heart of President Kennedy's social welfare program, consisting of bills for education, civil rights, depressed areas, minimum wage, emergency feed grains, housing, social security, water pollution, unemployment, and aid to dependent children. Liberalism in the context of this section, then, will refer to social and economic domestic issues. An examination of the fate of each bill in the House and the Senate, and, where appropriate, a comparison of the House version of the bill with the Senate version of the bill before Conference Committee, should provide a more precise comparison of liberalism between the two houses of Congress.[4] No attempt, however, has been made to weight the different provisions in each bill.

Two of the proposals are easily disposed of.

1. Aid to Education—passed by the Senate but rejected by the House. Senate considered more liberal.

2. Civil Rights Commission—by-passed committee hearings in the Senate for fear that the bill would never reach the floor. The House version was accepted on the floor of the Senate as an amendment to another bill. House considered more liberal.

The other eight issues require close inspection of the different versions before Conference Committee.

3. Depressed Areas—House bill before Conference Committee and Senate bill before Conference Committee similar except for two provisions in the House bill which were considered more liberal than Senate provisions (e.g., the House pro-

---

[3] *Ibid.*
[4] Data from the *Congressional Quarterly Almanac, ibid.*

vided for 100 per cent of the cost of loans under the provisions of the bill, the Senate, 65 per cent), and five provisions in the Senate bill which were considered more liberal than House provisions (e.g., financing the $300 million lending authority by direct Treasury financing rather than congressional appropriations as provided in the House version). Senate considered more liberal.

4. Minimum Wage—House and Senate bills before Conference Committee similar except in the following respects: House— raised minimum wage for those already covered to $1.15; Senate—raised to $1.25 in two years and two stages. House —workers newly covered, 1,300,000; Senate, 4,086,000. House—minimum wage for newly covered workers, $1.00; Senate—$1.25 in four steps over three years. House—no overtime for newly covered workers; Senate—most newly covered workers provided with overtime pay. On all four differing provisions the Senate may be considered more liberal than the House.

5. Emergency Feed Grains—nine differing provisions between the Senate and House versions of the bill before Conference Committee, five of which were considered more liberal in favor of the House (e.g., the market-sales provision in the House bill allowed the Secretary of Agriculture to flood the market with surplus grain, thereby driving down the price of the grain and hurting those who do not participate in the program [those who do participate in the program receive price supports]); four of the provisions were considered more liberal in favor of the Senate version (e.g., up to one-half of funds to be paid to farmers who retire crops from acreage may be paid in advance; no comparable provision in the House bill). Overall, House considered more liberal than the Senate.

6. Omnibus Housing—ten provisions in the House bill before Conference Committee considered to be more liberal (e.g., $100 million increase in direct loan fund for housing for

elderly as compared with $50 million provided by the Senate), and nine provisions in the Senate Bill before Conference Committee were considered to be more liberal (e.g., $80 million increase in urban planning grants as compared with $30 million provided by the House). The House bill also authorized more total funds for the housing program than did the Senate bill. House considered more liberal than the Senate.

7. Social Security—identical bills passed by the Senate and House before Conference Committee except for two liberalizing provisions in the Senate bill (increased ceiling on earnings, and temporary assistance for United States nationals returning home in distressed circumstances). Senate considered more liberal.

8. Water Pollution—House bill before Conference Committee contained three provisions considered more liberal than the Senate version (e.g., the House extended the administration's abatement plan for ten years, the Senate for five years), and the Senate bill contained two provisions considered more liberal than the House version (e.g., $25 million for research into new methods of sewage treatment). Overall, the House bill considered more liberal than the Senate.

9. Temporary Unemployment Benefits—four major differences between the House and Senate versions before Conference Committee, two increasing the liberalism of the House version (e.g., the Senate provided for reduced benefits to persons receiving pensions, the House did not), and two increasing the liberalism of the Senate version (e.g., the Senate provided a clause to increase the ceiling on federal grants, the House did not). Neither Senate nor House considered more liberal.

10. Aid to Dependent Children—the Senate added nine amendments to the House bill, five of them liberalizing the bill (e.g., increasing from 80 to 100 per cent the federal share

of costs of grants to states to train public welfare personnel), three of them reducing the liberal benefits provided by the House (e.g., postponed date for the Department of Health, Education, and Welfare's order cutting off federal funds from states that denied relief to children from "unsuitable" homes), and one indeterminate. Senate considered more liberal than the House.

Several interesting findings accrue from the above analysis. First, the Senate is by no means more liberal than the House on all bills. On certain issues, the House was considered more liberal than the Senate (civil rights, emergency feed grains, housing, and water pollution). Second, even on bills in which the Senate or the House, overall, was considered more liberal, the other house usually had several amendments which were more liberal. In summary, however, on the ten bills above, the Senate was considered to be more liberal on five, the House more liberal on four, and one indeterminate. Of the fifty-eight differing provisions in the eight bills which reached the Conference Committee, thirty-three, or 57 per cent, were liberalizing Senate amendments. Again the evidence, although by a narrow margin, indicates that the Senate is a more liberal body than the House. This detailed examination of ten important bills, together with the earlier data on Kennedy's total program, presents convincing evidence that the Senate is at least slightly more liberal than is the House.

WHY THE SENATE IS MORE LIBERAL THAN THE HOUSE

Two reasons are usually given for the fact that the Senate is likely to pass, on the whole, more liberal legislation than is the House. The first has to do with the manner in which the two houses are organized, the second with the kinds of constituencies the members of each house represent.

As to the first reason, the proposition that the Senate is more liberal than the House is supported in the following manner. The seniority rule in each house of Congress specifies that the committee members of the majority and minority parties who have been on the committee for the longest periods of continuous service are the chairman and the ranking minority member, respectively, of that committee. Also, important committee assignments and other leadership positions often go to members of each house who either have long periods of service or who can demonstrate that they are in no danger of being defeated at the polls.[5] Those members from less competitive districts, who are better able to gain seniority, are also more likely to come from districts with constituency characteristics more favorable to a conservative rather than a liberal position on many issues.[6]

Further, when the Democrats are in control of each house, southern members of the party, who tend to be less liberal than northern members,[7] have a disproportionate number of leadership positions. For example, in the Eighty-seventh Congress, although southern members represent only about 25 per cent of the total membership in each house, they chair, in each house, over 50 per cent of the committees. This disproportionate influence of the more conservative members in each house means that liberal positions supported by other members of Congress are not likely to prevail.

However, since the House of Representatives is considered, by most observers, to be more hierarchically organized than is the Senate (that is, leaders in the House have more power vis-à-vis other members than do Senate leaders),[8] the fact that leaders are

[5] With regard to committee assignments to the House Appropriations Committee, see Richard F. Fenno, Jr., "The House Appropriations Committee as a Political System: The Problem of Integration," *American Political Science Review,* LVI (June, 1962), 310–24.

For Committees in general, see Nicholas A. Masters, "House Committee Assignments, *American Political Science Review,* LV (June, 1961), 345–58. For a discussion of the seniority rule, see George Goodwin, Jr., "The Seniority System in Congress," *American Political Science Review,* LIII (June, 1959), 412–37.

[6] See Chapter 9 [of *Congressmen and Their Constituencies*] for evidence supporting this proposition.

[7] See Chapter 7 [of *Congressmen and Their Constituencies*].

[8] See William H. Riker, *Democracy in the United States* (New York: Macmillan, 1953), chap. v.

more conservative makes a bigger difference in the House than in the Senate. Given the more hierarchical power structure in the House, the positions supported by the more liberal non-leaders are even less likely to prevail than they are in the Senate. For these reasons, then, the public policies passed by the House will be more conservative than those passed by the Senate.

Although evidence for most of the above argument is fairly well established,[9] the weak link in the chain of the argument comes in the differences in liberalism-conservatism between leaders and non-leaders. Others report that there is little, or only slight evidence to indicate that the leaders of either house are more conservative than the rank-and-file.[10] As a further test of the hypothesis, representatives of the Eighty-seventh Congress, First Session were divided into leaders and non-leaders.[11] As a measure of liberalism in voting, the Larger Federal Role Support Score from the *Congressional Quarterly* was used.[12] As a measure of conservatism in voting, the Conservative Coalition Support Score from the *Congressional*

[9] Goodwin, *op. cit.*; Fenno, *op. cit.*; Lester W. Jackson, *District Safety, Seniority, and Chairmanships in the House of Representatives* (Unpublished Master's thesis, University of Wisconsin, 1961); and Chapters 7 and 9 of [*Congressmen and Their Constituencies*].

[10] See Duncan MacRae, Jr., *Dimensions of Congressional Voting* ("University of California Publication in Sociology and Social Institutions" [Berkeley: University of California Press, 1958]), I, 203–390, esp. pp. 289–98; David B. Truman, *The Congressional Party* (New York: Wiley, 1959), esp. chaps. iv and vi; and Goodwin, *op. cit.* Although Goodwin has no evidence on differences in liberalism between leaders and non-leaders, he does have data on party unity which indicate little difference between leaders and rank-and-file on party unity scores.

[11] Leaders include the majority leader and whip along with the twenty-one standing committee chairmen for the Democrats, and the minority leader and whip and twenty-one ranking minority members on the standing committees for the Republicans. Although the Speaker is also a party leader, he rarely votes. Hence, he is excluded from this analysis.

[12] See the *Congressional Quarterly Weekly Report,* No. 42, 1961, pp. 1751–63. The Larger Federal Role Index consists of ten House roll calls offering congressmen a choice between a larger or smaller federal role on various domestic issues.

TABLE 2

LIBERALISM AND CONSERVATISM SCORES OF LEADERS AND NON-LEADERS
IN THE HOUSE OF REPRESENTATIVES, 87TH CONGRESS, 1ST SESSION*

Members by Party	Average Scores†	
	Larger Federal Role	*Conservative Coalition Support*
Democrats		
Leaders	6.74	3.48
Non-Leaders	7.45	2.84
Republicans		
Leaders	1.20	6.65
Non-Leaders	1.24	6.95

* Data from the *Congressional Quarterly Weekly Report*, Nos. 42 and 44, 1961.

† Scales may vary from 0 to 9. Higher scores under Larger Federal Role indicate a greater degree of liberalism. Higher scores under Conservative Coalition Support indicate a greater degree of conservatism.

Quarterly was used.[13] Table 2 indicates that for Democrats, at least, the hypothesis is confirmed. Although the differences are relatively small, leaders of the Democratic party in the House do have a smaller average liberalism score and a higher average conservatism score than do non-leaders. (For the Republicans, the difference between leaders and non-leaders on the liberalism score is exceedingly small, and is in the wrong direction on the conservatism score.)[14]

[13] See *ibid.*, No. 44, 1961, pp. 1796–1806. The Conservative Coalition Support Index consists of twenty-three roll calls on which a majority of southern Democrats joined with a majority of Republicans in opposition to a majority of northern Democrats.

[14] Assuming this variable of leader, non-leader differences in liberalism-conservatism to be important in explaining differences in liberalism between the two houses, this may indicate that perhaps when the Republicans are in

The argument, then, that the House is more conservative than the Senate because of conservative leadership and greater hierarchical organization seems to be at least partially true, but the differences in liberalism-conservatism between leaders and non-leaders are so small that the question warrants investigation of additional explanations.

CONSTITUENCY DIFFERENCES AS A SECOND EXPLANATION

The second reason to be advanced in this chapter to explain why the Senate is more liberal than the House has to do with the nature of the constituencies which senators and congressmen represent. Senators, whose constituencies are entire states, are faced, on the whole, with more heterogeneous electorates than are congressmen, whose constituencies are smaller and likely to be more homogeneous. This is most obviously true for each state taken separately. The senators from that state have the entire state as their constituencies, congressmen only a portion of it (except for the eight states whose congressmen are elected at large).

The second explanation, then, for why the Senate is more liberal than the House will have two parts. First, we will show that certain population characteristics of congressional districts are associated with liberal and conservative voting records of congressmen.[15] We will then show that there are more House districts below than above the state average on population characteristics which are associated with liberalism, and more House districts above than below the state average on population characteristics which are associated with conservatism. Since the senators' constituencies are the state averages, if there are more congressional districts below the state averages on characteristics associated with liberalism and more congressional districts above the state averages on characteristics asso-

---

power, the Senate and the House will be more nearly equal in liberalism. This points up the need for comparative research on a number of Congresses.

[15] This point [is] explored further [in the following section].

ciated with conservatism, this will be evidence that one reason why the Senate is more liberal than the House has to do with the nature of the constituencies which senators and congressmen represent. Senators are more liberal because, on the whole, their constituencies have more of the characteristics associated with liberalism than do congressmen's constituencies.

The three population characteristics chosen for this study are (1) race (per cent non-white), (2) residence (per cent urban), and (3) socioeconomic status (per cent owner-occupied dwelling units).[16] Table 3 relates these population characteristics with voting in Congress. Congressmen from those districts which are below the state averages for percentage non-white and percentage urban were predicted to be less liberal than those congressmen from districts above the state averages for these two characteristics. Similarly, congressmen from those districts which are above the state averages for percentage owner-occupied dwelling units were also predicted to be less liberal. These hypotheses are fully consistent with the literature relating population characteristics with liberalism and conservatism. Non-white, urban, and lower socioeconomic groups are more likely to be liberal than their opposites (white, rural, and higher socioeconomic status groups).[17]

Table 3 illustrates that congressmen who come from districts

[16] Data for per cent non-white and per cent owner-occupied dwelling units come from the *Congressional District Data Book, Districts of the 87th Congress* (U.S. Department of Commerce, Bureau of the Census [Washington, D.C.: Government Printing Office, 1961]). Data for per cent urban come from the *Congressional Quarterly Weekly Report,* No. 8, 1962. The definition of urban area is that of the Bureau of the Census, 1960.

[17] See, for example, Seymour M. Lipset, Paul F. Lazarsfeld, Allen H. Barton, and Juan Linz, "The Psychology of Voting: An Analysis of Political Behavior," in Gardner Lindzey, ed., *Handbook of Social Psychology* (Cambridge, Mass.: Addison-Wesley, 1954), pp. 1124–77; Bernard Berelson, Paul F. Lazarsfeld, and William N. McPhee, *Voting* (Chicago: University of Chicago Press, 1954); and Angus Campbell, Philip E. Converse, Warren E. Miller, and Donald E. Stokes, *The American Voter* (New York: Wiley, 1960).

TABLE 3

LIBERALISM SCORES FOR CONGRESSMEN WHO COME FROM DISTRICTS ABOVE
AND BELOW STATE AVERAGES ON THREE POPULATION CHARACTERISTICS*

	Mean Average Scores† Congressional Districts			
Population Characteristics	*Above* State Average	N	*Below* State Average	N
Per Cent Non-White	6.22	(155)	4.14	(264)
Per Cent Urban	5.52	(191)	4.44	(232)
Per Cent Owner-Occupied Dwelling Units	4.07	(248)	6.16	(175)

* Data compiled from the *Congressional District Data Book, Districts of the 87th Congress* (U.S. Department of Commerce, Bureau of the Census [Washington, D.C.: Government Printing Office, 1961]), *Congressional Quarterly Weekly Report*, No. 8, 1962, and the *Congressional Quarterly Weekly Report*, No. 42, 1961.

† Liberalism averages are based on the Larger Federal Role Index. Mean averages may vary from 0 to 9, a larger average denoting a higher degree of liberalism.

below the state averages on percentage non-white and percentage urban, and above the state averages on percentage owner-occupied dwelling units are less liberal than their opposites.

Table 3 also illustrates that there are more congressional districts which are below the state averages on characteristics associated with liberalism than above the state averages, and more House districts above the state averages on population characteristics associated with conservatism than below the state averages. There are more districts below the state averages for percentage non-white than above (264 to 155), more districts below the state averages on percentage urban than above (232 to 191), and more districts above the state averages for percentage owner-occupied units than below (248 to 175). Since the state averages are the senators' districts, and there are more House districts below the state averages on population characteristics associated with liberalism than above the state averages, and more House districts above the state averages on population characteristics associated with conservatism than below the state averages, we may conclude that this difference in the kinds of constituencies which are represented in the two houses provides additional explanation of why the Senate is more liberal than the House.

We have been concerned, in this chapter, with a dual question: Is the Senate more liberal than the House of Representatives, and, if so, why? We presented two sets of data to support the proposition that the Senate is more liberal than the House. The first set analyzed the fate of 322 bills personally supported by President Kennedy. We found that Senate committee and floor action was more likely to be favorable and less likely to be unfavorable than House committee and floor action in the handling of these bills. Assuming that President Kennedy is a liberal and that the legislative program he submits to Congress will, by and large, be a liberal program, this data was considered evidence that the Senate is more liberal than the House.

The second set of data concerned ten of President Kennedy's most important requests for domestic welfare legislation. We found that the Senate versions of these bills before Conference Committee were, on the whole, more likely than the House versions to be liberal in orientation. This more detailed examination using more elaborate criteria of liberalism-conservatism provided additional evidence that the Senate is more liberal than the House.

In answering the question of why the Senate is more liberal than the House, we found two explanations to be useful. The first had to do with structural reasons, the second with the kinds of constituencies which senators and representatives tend to represent. We found leaders to be slightly more conservative than non-leaders, and this fact, coupled with the hypothesis that the House is more hierarchically organized than the Senate, provides one explanation. Given the differences in organization between the two houses, and the differences in policy preferences between leaders and non-leaders, these organizational differences help us to explain why the Senate is more likely to support liberal legislation than is the House.

The second reason why the Senate is more liberal than the House concerned the differences in constituencies represented in each house. We found that there are more House districts below state averages on population characteristics associated with liberalism than above state averages (percentage non-white and percentage urban), and more House districts above state averages on population characteristics associated with conservatism than below state averages (percentage owner-occupied dwelling units). Since the senators' districts are the state averages, these data provided an additional explanation of why the Senate is more liberal than the House. Not only does the manner in which the houses are organized make a difference, but also the kinds of constituencies which are represented in each house. Both institutional factors and factors exogenous to the institution were helpful in our explanation.

Constituency Differences between Parties and Congressional Roll-Call Voting

[Our next concern is] with the relationships among constituency factors, party differences, and congressional voting. This interest follows from a prior concern with one of the most important problems in democratic government, to wit, the relationship between the preferences of the governed and the outcomes of governmental processes. In democratic governments, we would expect to find some degree of relationship between how representatives of the people act on matters of public policy and the kinds of people who are being represented. Studies of legislatures provide fertile field for such explorations, since legislators usually represent different, relatively small segments of the population.

An argument is not being made here that the way congressmen vote on bills on the floor of Congress is the only factor which determines the course of public policy. Besides the obvious fact that the President, executive agencies, and the courts must also be taken into account in any complete examination of the policy-making process, exclusive reliance on roll-call voting by legislators ignores the influence of other important legislative processes. Many bills introduced in Congress, for example, never reach the floor for a vote. Of President Kennedy's 355 legislative requests in 1961, less than half reached the floor of both houses for a vote.[18] Or, more generally, of the 3,071 bills and resolutions introduced in the Senate in the First Session of the Eighty-seventh Congress, about one-third, or 1,133 were passed. In the House of Representatives, which does not allow multiple sponsorship of the same bill (and hence encourages many members to sponsor identical bills), 10,955 bills and resolutions introduced in 1961 resulted in 1,234 being passed.[19]

Not only do considerably less than half of the total number of bills and resolutions introduced in Congress reach the floor, but those that do make the floor-debate stage are often considerably different bills and resolutions than when first introduced. Most of the disparity between the number and content of bills introduced in Congress and bills which reach the floor for debate may be accounted for by the power of congressional committees and their ability to stop, impede, alter, modify, or report out unchanged legislation which is submitted to them. Hence, a study of congressional decision-making which concentrates on roll-call voting leaves out of consideration the important influences which congressional committees have on the kind of legislation which is likely to get through Congress.[20]

[18] See the *Congressional Quarterly Almanac* (Washington, D.C.: Congressional Quarterly, Inc., 1961), Vol. XVII.

[19] Floyd M. Riddick, "The Eighty-seventh Congress: First Session," *Western Political Quarterly*, XV (June, 1962), 254–74.

[20] See, for example, Charles O. Jones, "The Role of the Congressional Sub-Committee," *Midwest Journal of Political Science*, VI (November, 1962), 327–45; Richard Fenno, *op. cit.*, 310–24; Charles O. Jones, "Representation in Congress: The Case of the House Agriculture Committee," *American Political Science Review*, LV (June, 1961), 358–68; and Ralph K. Huitt, "The Congressional Committee: A Case Study," *American Political Science Review*, XLVIII (June, 1954), 340–65.

Recognizing this limitation, however, merely means that all influences on the legislative process are not being considered here. It does not mean that the conclusions reached in this study are therefore invalid. The bills which do reach the floor of Congress for debate and roll-call vote are often quite important pieces of legislation, and a majority vote, of course, is needed in each house for passage. Roll-call voting is an important stage in the legislative process, then, and interested citizens will be concerned with the outcome of the voting. How different congressmen representing different kinds of constituencies vote on these bills, therefore, ought to give us some clue as to the importance of constituency and other influences in the legislative process. These influences may be working in other important stages of legislative decision-making, but they will also be prominent at the voting stage.

Having said this, what is the relationship between roll-call votes of congressmen and their constituencies? Can certain patterns of voting be discerned which will aid us in the understanding of the representative process? What follows is an attempt to answer these questions.

THE IMPORTANCE OF PARTY

Studies of roll-call voting in Congress have tended to stress two factors: (1) the large amount of party cohesion in Congress on most issues, and (2) the importance of constituency factors in explaining deviations from party votes within parties.[21] These studies suggest that party is the single most important predictor of roll-call behavior, and that constituency factors explain most of the deviation from party votes.[22] For example, Turner suggests that:

[21] Julius Turner, *Party and Constituency: Pressures on Congress* ("The Johns Hopkins University Studies in Historical and Political Science," Series 69, No. 1 [Baltimore: The Johns Hopkins Press, 1951]); MacRae, *op. cit.*, pp. 203–390; and Truman, *op. cit.* For an analysis of variability on issues, see MacRae, *op. cit.*, and Samuel C. Patterson, "Dimensions of Voting Behavior in a One-Party State Legislature," *Public Opinion Quarterly*, XXVI (Summer, 1962), 185–201.
[22] Other factors include leaders versus rank-and-file, and state delegations, see Truman, *op. cit.*

quantitative analysis of roll-call votes shows, contrary to majority opinion, that significant differences exist between our major parties. While it is true that American discipline falls short of that achieved in some European democracies, and is less effective than party discipline in the McKinley era in the United States, evidence of great party influence can still be found. Party pressure seems to be more effective than any other pressure on congressional voting. . . .[23]

The extent of party unity can be seen from an analysis of roll-call votes in various Congresses. In 1961, 58 per cent of the 320 roll calls in both the Senate and the House found a majority of Democrats opposing a majority of Republicans. In 1960, 1959, 1958, and 1957 the comparable percentages were 42, 50, 42, and 47, respectively.[24] Certainly, as Turner points out, this is less than might be found in European systems, but it does give some indication that political parties do provide a basis of cleavage in American politics.

However, taking 1961 as an example (in which 58 per cent of the roll-call votes were votes on which a majority of one party opposed a majority of the other party), this still leaves 42 per cent, 135 out of 320, of the roll-call votes without a majority of Democrats opposing a majority of Republicans. Also, the average Democratic and Republican representative in both the Senate and the House voted only about 70 per cent of the time in agreement with his party on the 185 roll-call votes in which a majority of one party opposed a majority of the other party.[25] This means that on 30 per cent of these votes, the average Democrat and Republican voted against the majority of his party.

How does one explain this degree of party unity within Congress? How does one account for the extent of party deviation among congressmen? This [section] will attempt to demonstrate a relationship between party membership of congressmen and constituency factors and to show how variation in such constituency

[23] Turner, *op. cit.,* p. 23.
[24] *Congressional Quarterly Weekly Report,* No. 49, 1961, p. 1929.
[25] *Ibid.*

factors influences congressional voting. It will attempt to demonstrate that differences between Democrats and Republicans are not merely a matter of party label or ideology (few really contend otherwise), but are rooted in basic differences in the kinds of constituencies from which Democrats and Republicans come. . . . [This section] will then go on to show that these constituency factors are also important in explaining intraparty differences in voting in Congress, but only by way of supporting the hypothesis that party voting patterns reflect constituency differences.

This analysis is rooted in the general theory [already] described. That is, people located in similar kinds of environments are likely to share similar attitudes, such as voting Democratic or Republican, and to differ in their attitudes from those who do not share similar environmental situations. Hence, we would expect Democratic and Republican congressmen to disagree on a number of important public policy questions, and that these party differences will be reflected in different environmental conditions between Democratic and Republican constituencies. That is, as we will attempt to demonstrate, differences in congressional voting between Democrats and Republicans also reflect differences in gross kinds of political pressures.

Party and Constituency Differences on Public Policy

The first step in our analysis is to demonstrate voting differences between Democrats and Republicans on matters of public policy. We will concentrate, in most of what follows, on differences between Democrats and Republicans in the northern and border states, excluding the 101 southern Democrats and 5 southern Republicans of the Old Confederacy. It was found, on preliminary analysis of the data, that although southern congressmen did exhibit distinctly different voting patterns from northern congressmen (see Table 4), the gross constituency variables chosen for this analysis did not show a relationship with voting in Congress among the southern congressmen. Other variables than the ones chosen in this study will have to be employed to explain differences in southern congressional voting.

Our unit of analysis will be the House of Representatives, Eighty-seventh Congress, First Session. The findings in this [section] are, of course, limited by time (one Congress) and place (the House of Representatives). It is hoped that the findings and explanations reported here will stimulate further research on other legislative bodies.

The best single source describing differences between the voting records of Democrats and Republicans is the *Congressional Quar-*

TABLE 4

SCORES OF NORTHERN DEMOCRATS, SOUTHERN DEMOCRATS, AND NORTHERN REPUBLICANS ON THREE SERIES OF ROLL-CALL VOTES*

	Average Scores			
Region and Party	*Kennedy Domestic Support* %	*Kennedy Foreign Support* %	*Larger Federal Role* %	*Total* N
Northern Democrats	83.8	83.9	92.7	(163)
Southern Democrats	56.9	57.2	56.4	(101)
Northern Republicans	34.4	53.3	17.3	(168)

* Data compiled from the *Congressional Quarterly Weekly Report*, Nos. 42, 45, 1961.

terly. We will use three of its groupings of votes: the Kennedy Support Score on Domestic Policy (percentage support on fifty roll-call votes on matters of domestic policy which President Kennedy personally favored); the Kennedy Support Score on Foreign Policy (percentage support on fifteen roll-call votes on matters of foreign policy which President Kennedy personally favored); and the Larger Federal Role Support Score (percentage support on ten roll-call votes which would increase the federal government's role in various aspects of our economy and society, e.g., aid to education, housing, minimum wage).[26] Table 4 presents the voting of northern Democrats, southern Democrats, and northern Republicans on these three indices.

Table 4 shows striking differences in voting patterns between northern Democrats, southern Democrats, and northern Republicans. The average Kennedy Support Score on Domestic Policy for northern Democrats is 83.8 per cent, for southern Democrats, 56.9 per cent, and for northern Republicans, 34.4 per cent; on Foreign Policy, 83.9 per cent for northern Democrats, 57.2 per cent for southern Democrats, and 53.3 per cent for northern Republicans. Northern Democrats support a Larger Federal Role 92.7 per cent of the time, southern Democrats, 56.4 per cent, and northern Republicans, 17.3 per cent. In each case, the southern Democrats lie somewhere between the average scores of northern Democrats and Republicans.

The second step in our argument is to illustrate constituency differences between Northern Democrats and northern Republicans. The variables we have chosen are socioeconomic status (percentage owner-occupied dwelling units), race (percentage non-white population), population density (average population per square mile), and place of residence (percentage urban).[27] We expect, and find, that northern Democrats tend to come from districts which have a smaller percentage owner-occupied dwelling units, a higher percentage non-white population, a higher average population per square mile, and a higher percentage urban population than do northern Republicans. Table 5 presents these data.

We now have grounds for saying that one of the reasons why northern Democrats vote differently from northern Republicans in

[26] *Congressional Quarterly Weekly Report,* Nos. 42, 45, 1961.

[27] Data from the *Congressional District Data Book, Districts of the 87th Congress* (U.S. Department of Commerce, Bureau of the Census [Washington, D.C.: Government Printing Office, 1961]) for the first three variables, and the *Congressional Quarterly Weekly Report,* No. 8, 1962, for percentage urban. The definition of "urban" is that used by the Bureau of the Census, 1960.

the House of Representatives is that the congressmen from each party tend to represent different kinds of constituencies. Northern Democratic constituencies are more urban, more racially mixed, have a lower percentage of owner-occupied dwelling units, and have more people per square mile than northern Republican constituencies. In other words, factors which are usually associated with liberalism (urban, lower socio-economic status, non-white,

TABLE 5

COMPARISON BETWEEN NORTHERN DEMOCRATS AND NORTHERN REPUBLICANS ON FOUR CONSTITUENCY VARIABLES*

Region and Party	Mean Average of Constituency Variables				
	Owner-Occupied %	Non-White %	Pop./ Sq. Mile Av.	Urban %	Total N
Northern† Democrat	55.5	12.6	11,032	74.5	(163)
Northern Republican	67.1	3.8	1,667	65.1	(168)

* Data compiled from the *Congressional District Data Book*, *Districts of the 87th Congress* (U.S. Department of Commerce, Bureau of the Census [Washington, D.C.: Government Printing Office, 1962]), and the *Congressional Quarterly Weekly Report*, No. 8, 1962.

† Northern includes all but the eleven former Confederate states.

and densely populated areas) are the factors which are, in fact, associated with the more liberal party. And, if we assume that Kennedy is a liberal and that his program submitted to Congress is a liberal program, Table 6 illustrates that each of these four characteristics is correlated with a more liberal voting record, even with party held constant.

Table 6 shows the following relationships for both northern Democrats and northern Republicans: The lower the percentage of owner-occupied dwelling units in the congressional districts, the higher the Kennedy Support Score on Domestic Policy; the higher

TABLE 6

RELATIONSHIP BETWEEN FOUR CONSTITUENCY FACTORS AND KENNEDY SUPPORT SCORE ON DOMESTIC POLICY FOR NORTHERN DEMOCRATS AND NORTHERN REPUBLICANS*

Region and Party	Domestic Policy Score and Constituency Factors				
	% Owner-Occupied $\phi\dagger$	% Non-White ϕ	Pop./ Sq. Mile ϕ	% Urban ϕ	Total N
Northern Democrats	−.13	.19	.23	.26	(163)
Northern Republicans	−.12	.08	.05	.20	(168)

* Data compiled from the *Congressional Quarterly Weekly Report*, No. 42, 1961, and No. 8, 1962, and the *Congressional District Data Book*, *Districts of the 87th Congress* (U.S. Department of Commerce, Bureau of the Census [Washington, D.C.: Government Printing Office, 1961]).

† The measure of association is the phi coefficient.

the percentage non-white population per square mile, and percentage urban, the higher the Kennedy Support Score on Domestic Policy. The correlations are smaller for Republicans than for Democrats, but all are in the predicted direction.

We can now sum up our argument to this point. First, northern Democrats have more liberal voting records than do Republicans. Second, Democrats tend to come from districts with larger proportions of characteristics which are generally associated with liberalism than do Republicans. Third, these constituency differences are associated with liberal voting records independent of political party.

Hence, Democrats have more liberal voting records partially, at least, because they tend to come from more liberal constituencies.

Finally, our argument can be bolstered in the following way: We can combine the four constituency variables into a single index. This is done by splitting each constituency variable at the median and separating those constituencies that are above the median on none, one, two, three, and four of the variables (for percentage owner-occupied dwelling units, above the median means scoring low on this characteristic). This index is then related to the party affiliation of the incumbent representatives. We predicted that as the number of characteristics above the median increased, there would be a higher proportion of Democrats elected. Table 7 presents data testing this hypothesis.

The data in Table 7 illustrate the proposition that whether a

TABLE 7

NORTHERN DEMOCRATS AND REPUBLICANS ON COMBINED
CONSTITUENCY INDEX*

Number of Characteristics above the Median	Party		Total N
	Democratic %	Republican %	
0	38	62	(55)
1	43	57	(89)
2	37	63	(52)
3	53	47	(70)
4	74	26	(65)

* The point biserial correlation for these data is .23.

Democratic or Republican congressman is elected from a constituency is in considerable measure related to the four gross constituency factors which we have been considering. With one exception, as the number of characteristics above the median increases, the percentage of Democratic incumbents increases. At the extremes, of the fifty-five congressional districts which, relatively speaking, have the most conservative population characteristics, 62 per cent elected a Republican congressman in 1960. And, of the sixty-five congressional districts which, again relatively speaking, have the most liberal population characteristics, 74 per cent elected a Democratic congressman in 1960.

Not only do those districts we have defined as liberal tend to elect Democrats and those districts we have defined as conservative tend to elect Republicans, but these constituency differences have effects on the behavior of the particular Democrats and Republicans who are elected, as well. For example, combining, for purposes of this analysis, those constituencies whose scores were none, only one, or only two above the median as conservative constituencies, and those constituencies whose scores were three or all four above the median as liberal constituencies, among the Democrats who come from conservative districts, 25 per cent have a Kennedy Support Score on Domestic Policy of 90 per cent or better. Among the Democrats who come from liberal districts, 41 per cent have a Kennedy Support Score on Domestic Policy of 90 per cent or better. Similarly, among the Republicans who come from liberal districts, 72 per cent support Kennedy more than 30 per cent of the time; whereas among the Republicans who come from conservative districts, only 58 per cent score this high.

This contrast is made even stronger when we look at the differences in voting on a select group of issues on which a majority of Republicans sided with a majority of southern Democrats against a majority of northern Democrats. This is the so-called Conservative Coalition.[28] Among the Democrats who come from conservative districts, 81 per cent voted with the Conservative Coalition on at least one of these twenty-three issues. Among the Democrats who come from liberal districts, only 31 per cent ever voted with the coalition. Similarly, among the Republicans who come from liberal

[28] *Congressional Quarterly Weekly Report,* No. 44, 1961.

districts, 56 per cent voted with the Conservative Coalition at least 70 per cent of the time. Among the Republicans who come from conservative districts, 75 per cent voted with the coalition at least 70 per cent of the time.

We may conclude, then, that much of the difference in roll-call votes between northern Democrats and northern Republicans may be explained on the basis of relationships between certain constituency characteristics and tendencies to vote liberal or conservative (these relationships hold even with party held constant). The fact that liberal districts tend to produce Democrats and conservative districts, Republicans, completes the argument.

ADDITIONAL SPECULATION

We are also left with a speculative notion of this nature: It might be quite possible that the relationships between constituency factors, party affiliation of congressmen, and roll-call votes would be even higher than here indicated if we knew something of the congressman's perception of his district and what he considers to be his effective constituency.[29] Perhaps Democratic congressmen from the North tend to overrepresent the liberal elements within their constituencies because those are the ones which they perceive (and perhaps quite rightly) as being important for their election and re-election. Similarly, it might be the case that Republican congressmen tend to overrepresent the conservative elements within their constituencies for the same reasons. This selective attention to groups within a constituency would help to explain why the correlation between gross constituency factors and party affiliation of the winning candidate is not stronger than here indicated. The fact that gross constituency variables explain as much as they do is note-

[29] For a discussion of the importance of perception in the representative-constituency relationship, see Lewis A. Dexter, "The Representative and His District," *Human Organization,* XVI (Spring, 1957), 11–16. For initial data on the problem, see Warren E. Miller, "Policy Preferences of Congressional Candidates and Constituents," Paper delivered at the 1961 Annual Meeting of The American Political Association, St. Louis, Missouri.

worthy, but the addition of data about congressmen's perceptions of their constituencies and the probable differential attention to and access by some groups rather than others would help us to understand better the representative relationship between the congressman and his constituency.

A related point has to do with the "responsible parties" question. Turner has pointed out that because of the heterogeneous make-up of the parties, attempts to enforce a more rigid party line in Congress might have the effect of forcing many congressmen to take positions inconsistent with constituency influences. This, in Turner's view, would have the effect of reducing the strength of the party in those areas and increasing the number of one-party areas.[30] The data reported here are consistent with Turner's views. Democrats from conservative-type districts and Republicans from liberal-type districts do tend to vote more conservatively and liberally respectively than their party cohorts. Forcing a stricter party line on these congressmen might indeed affect their ability to please their own constituents, reduce their strength within their own constituencies, and increase the number of one-party districts.

One further note about the methodology used in this [section]: The measures and data employed are admittedly gross. This leaves a great deal of room for error. But, as far as possible, in choosing data and methods we have attempted to load the dice against the hypotheses rather than for them. For example, the states excluded from the analysis are the eleven former Confederate states only. Included in the definition of northern states are Kentucky, Oklahoma, and other border states. Similarly, we have used as our most important measure of voting differences the Kennedy Support Score on Domestic Policy, an index which, if anything, would tend to maximize party differences over a wide range of issues because of the direct involvement in such issues by a Democratic President. And, third, the constituency variables included in this analysis are limited in number and, again, are of the grossest variety. Still, un-

[30] Julius Turner, "Responsible Parties: A Dissent from the Floor," *American Political Science Review,* XLV (March, 1951), 143–52.

der all these limiting conditions, the major hypothesis of this [section] that voting differences between Democrats and Republicans reflect, at least in part, constituency differences between Democrats and Republicans is substantiated. Further, more specific, research into the relationship between constituency influence and congressional voting should help us to estimate more precisely how important such influence is in relation to other factors.

Congress and Foreign Policy

Robert A. Dahl

In the selection that follows, Professor Dahl erects three criteria which we may use to evaluate the adequacy of the process by which all public policy is made. The process should insure that the leadership is responsible, that is, that its policies are based upon the wishes of the electorate; the process should facilitate agreement so that policy grows out of full and clarifying discussion; and the process should eventuate in rational decisions. The goals of an adequate policy process, then, are responsibility, agreement, and rationality.

The steady accretion of power in executive hands, long noted and even applauded by analysts of American government, has been severe in domestic policy and even more drastic in foreign policy. Indeed, the response of the American system of government to the pressures of world events in recent decades has raised

SOURCE: Robert A. Dahl, *Congress and Foreign Policy* (New York: Harcourt, Brace & World, 1950), chs. 8 and 13, pp. 107–19, 205–19. Copyright 1950, by Harcourt, Brace & World, Inc., and reprinted with their permission.

the genuine possibility of converting the President into a kind of constitutional dictator in the realm of foreign policy.

The beginnings of this development lie deeply buried in the American past, and some of them derive from the exigencies so frequently present in foreign policy and absent in domestic policy. Foreign policy *is* different from domestic policy and those differences serve to enhance executive power, as Thomas Jefferson both noted and demonstrated.

But to discern this fact is not to condemn us to accept a constitutional dictatorship in foreign affairs and its accompanying erosion of congressional power. It is to assert rather that the adequacy of the process by which foreign policy is made must be constantly scrutinized and kept in harmony with democratic purposes.

If the adequacy of that process is to be measured by the criteria of responsibility, agreement, and rationality, Professor Dahl argues, then there must be a revitalization of the congressional role in foreign policy making. This will in turn require some internal changes within Congress to enable it to perform more effectively in the realm of foreign policy. Reversal of the historic trend of distribution of power is not easy, but the result of the continuance of the present evolution is both discernible and undesirable.

At a time when the country is passing through a crisis of quite dangerous dimensions, during which the adequacy of our foreign policy process is central to that crisis, this argument is both cogent and attractive. As America went to the polls to choose a new President in 1968, powerful voices insisted that, at least in Asia, our policy was not responsive to the preferences of the electorate; its very rationality was widely questioned, and President Johnson's withdrawal was eloquent testimony that the consensus necessary to sustain so important and burdensome a policy had been decisively sundered.

Moreover, it was not merely a given policy that was in question but the acceptability of the process by which that policy had been developed. Perhaps at no time since the McCarthyite period of the early 1950's had the political atmosphere been so poisoned, and the legitimacy of an administration so impaired, as by the charges of a "credibility gap" in the conduct of foreign policy.

The congressional role in the struggle over the foreign policy process, particularly that of the Senate which is made the senior partner by the Constitution, has conditioned and prepared our politics for a fresh determination, and perhaps a new departure, in the method by which our foreign policy is made. A succession of Presidents have borne in mind the tragic failure of Wilson to count the Congress as a partner in his determination to join the League of Nations. It is unlikely that the bitter lessons of Vietnam will be lost on Mr. Johnson's successors. But before the Congress can be utilized in the pursuit of responsibility, agreement, and rationality, the reasons for its eclipse and the bases of its restoration must be determined. To this end the selection from Professor Dahl makes a significant contribution.

A Constitutional Dictator?

A prince who wishes to maintain the state, Machiavelli reminds us, is often forced to do evil. Is this the case with the American President?

[We have seen] that Congressional prerogatives stipulated by constitutional theory and practice stand directly athwart presidential supremacy in foreign affairs. But one may easily fall into error by assuming that constitutional prerogative is the equivalent of power. Is it not possible that in foreign policy the executive can take the substance of power and leave Congress the shadow? If Congressional consent is required by certain widely accepted constitutional stipulations, cannot the President use the powers of the executive-administrative to feed foreign policy into one end of the Congressional hopper and run it through the formalities of the lawmaking process without significant change? Or to put it differently: Whoever can decisively affect the Congressman's preferences or his views of reality can substantially control his voting behavior. Does the executive-administrative have at its disposal adequate means for influencing the Congressman's preferences and reality views on questions of foreign policy?

The argument [here] is that the executive-administrative does indeed possess some important means of this kind. Any realistic examination of the power relationships existing between President and Congress must take these influences into account. It may well be that the dynamic of events will strengthen these influences to the point where the Chief Executive is a kind of constitutional dictator in foreign policy. But this is not to say that the constitutional dictator is the only alternative still open to us, nor that it is the most preferable, assuming the values of rationality, responsibility, and agreement. . . .

MOBILIZING PUBLIC OPINION

The President may—indeed often does—attempt to manipulate the Congressman's preferences and opportunities for re-election by mobilizing public opinion behind his own policies.

In domestic policy this practice dates at least from Jackson's administration, when the President sought to use public opinion as a weapon against Congress in the conflict over the Bank. It is perhaps worth recalling, however, that although Jackson was re-elected in 1832, even that popular President failed to gain a favorable Congress and therefore had to resort to his executive powers to achieve his ends.

In foreign policy, the use of public opinion as a force in the President's struggle with Congress is a weapon too ready at hand to be underestimated. It should not be overly difficult for the executive branch to create a "crisis" in foreign affairs by the release of appropriate information at its disposal. Lincoln Steffens tells us in his autobiography that as a police reporter in New York he created a local "crime wave" merely by a somewhat more intensive reporting of crimes than had theretofore been the practice. It is perhaps not too much to expect that the executive branch, by withholding or releasing information at its disposal and by its silence or its public statements, may significantly influence public impressions as to whether or not a serious crisis in foreign relations exists at any given moment or in any given area. There are, to be sure, limits within which the picture of reality can be manipulated, but within these limits executive decisions can sometimes play a decisive role.[1]

Thus in the postwar period the executive evidently began to play up an interpretation of events in Europe as a crisis which the United States had to meet with definite foreign policy measures; and at the same time, it played down—until much later—such an interpretation of events in China. Congressmen and others who sought release of the suppressed Wedemeyer report on China were probably right in their belief that the report would have an impact on public opinion about our China policy roughly comparable to the impact on public opinion of speeches and comments by members of the executive on the need for a new American policy for Europe. In retrospect it seems clear that had the executive chosen to do so, by co-operating with events it could have created a popular sense of crisis over happenings in the Far East more nearly like the one developing at that time over European events.

But in the strategy and generalship of foreign relations how useful is the technique of manipulating Congress through public opinion? As a method of overcoming deadlock, a presidential appeal to public opinion is not without practical difficulties. Short of waiting for another election, it is sometimes difficult to know how the various publics have made up their minds. Public opinion polls, letters, or newspaper editorials may not be influential in breaking the deadlock. And in various respects these may distort the way in which the various publics will act on election day or when concrete sacrifices are demanded in behalf of the policy. Yet to sit back and wait for the next election is to play into the hands of crisis. Even the election may not resolve the conflict; given the separation of powers and a weak party structure, the election may only return both contestants in the controversy. At least for domestic policy, this appears to have been the case in the elections of 1948.

Or the President's appeal may be rejected, as was President Wil-

[1] William L. Neumann, "How to Merchandise Foreign Policy," *American Perspective,* September and October, 1949, pp. 183–93, 235–50. See also Homer Bigart, "State Department's News Policy," New York *Herald Tribune,* Jan. 10, 1950, p. 22.

son's demand for a Democratic Congress in 1918. If the President is engaged in negotiations, this defeat may place him in a most delicate situation, particularly today when the executive-Congressional relationship is much better understood in foreign chancelleries than it evidently was in 1918.

If the technique is to be successfully employed, therefore, the executive branch must be given such a superiority of means for manipulating public opinion that it would regularly emerge the winner in any executive-Congressional conflict. There are values according to which such a development might be justified. But they are not the values of a democratic society.

STATE DEPARTMENT AS WARD HEELER

There are other methods of manipulating Congress short of a drastic control of public opinion, and these are a part of the traditional practice of executive relations with Congress. In various ways the executive branch may apply gentle pressures on Congressmen: the President may employ patronage; the Departments may provide certain helpful services to members of Congress; influential pressure groups under executive influence may be brought into action; the favorite projects of certain members of Congress may be looked on with more tolerance. These are all devices that have grown up as essentially irrational substitutes for the more rational executive-Congressional relationship that is inhibited by the separation of powers. From a democratic point of view, the techniques are decidedly unattractive, for they secure legislative action through influences that have no necessary relationship to the wants and desires of the electorate. But such influences undoubtedly help to grease the squeaking wheels of constitutional machinery designed rather for maintaining the power of minorities within a negative state than for meeting the needs of majorities in the modern, positive state.

Yet even as a *pis aller,* this technique for manipulating Congress has limited utility in the operation of foreign policy. For one thing, the techniques may bring about an empty victory unless Congress and the public *are* genuinely behind the policy. To develop an arrangement that will insure a positive relation between public policy and public support is the basic problem, not the mere winning of temporary executive victories over Congress.

Congress has a way of taking its revenge on the executive when it is manipulated into consenting legislatively to a policy that it does not really endorse. It may harass the executive by investigations, by using the appropriations process to weaken the organization or to secure policy changes, by legislating certain personnel out of office, and if need be by modifying the statute itself. The perennial phenomenon of Congress delegating power with one hand and retaking it with the other, which leads to so much instability in policy and administration, probably stems in part from the fact that the original delegation was secured less because of basic agreement on policy than because of the manipulative techniques customarily employed by the executive in getting policies approved.

An even more important limitation on these techniques is the weakness of the State Department as an instrument for this kind of manipulation. To begin with, the Department has very few personal services it can provide for individual Congressmen. To be sure, there are some. It can facilitate passports.[2] Foreign Service officers abroad can provide special assistance to Congressional delegations or individual Congressmen and their families.[3] The State Depart-

[2] Witness the following encomiums by Democratic and Republican members of the House Appropriations Subcommittee:

"Mr. O'BRIEN. Mr. Chairman, I should like to say for Mrs. Shipley [Chief of the Passport Division] that she is the most accommodating person, man or woman, in Government service, has been certainly to Members of Congress; and I am willing to vote anything Mrs. Shipley says she needs for her office.

"Mr. STEFAN. I think we all agree with Mr. O'Brien's comment concerning Mrs. Shipley."

(*Department of State Appropriation Bill for 1949: Hearings before the Subcommittee of the Committee on Appropriations*, House of Representatives, 80th Cong., 2d sess., pp. 155–56.)

[3] Representative Karl Stefan, chairman of the House Appropriations Subcommittee on the State Department, stated in the 1948 hearings: "In my forty-five-odd years of traveling around the world, I have had the pleasure of meeting a great many of our employees who represent the Government in various capacities, especially Foreign Service officers . . . it is a great inspiration to get into a little bit of American land in foreign countries, and

ment may also write speeches for Congressmen, a service all government departments are happy to perform. It is well authenticated that more than one member of Congress has acquired a reputation for a profound understanding of foreign policy on the basis of speeches written for him by the State Department; occasionally a member is even "built up" into something of a figure by the solicitous coaching of State Department Officials.

Services such as these may help;[4] but they cannot overcome the real weakness of the Department as a player in *this* kind of political game. The State Department has virtually no "constituency." It is not the kind of service agency whose benefits are immediately visible to important voting blocs; therefore it cannot easily mobilize citizen pressures on Congress. In this respect, it differs fundamentally from the Department of Agriculture, which as a service agency to farmers is a political power in its own right; or the Department of Labor with its services to trade-unions and workers; or the Department of Commerce with its services to businessmen; or the Department of Interior with its variegated services to electric power consumers, irrigated areas, reclamation districts, and the like. Citi-

---

there meet an American who has his finger on the pulse of the country in which he is serving us as our representative. . . . To see these Americans typify America, the American way of life, and transmit it to these foreign people was a great inspiration to me." (*Dept. of State Approp. Bill for 1949, Hearings,* pp. 314–15.) Representative Stefan's enthusiasm did not, however, prevent a cut in the Foreign Service appropriation for that year.

[4] Congressman Ramspeck, at that time majority whip in the House, testified in 1945 on the basis of his intimate observation of Congress since 1911: ". . . actually the executive branch of the Government has come to wield more and more influence over the legislative branch, because we have undertaken to do things for our constituents which put us under obligation to the executive branch of the Government. It is fine to talk about not being influenced by those sorts of things, but if you go down to a department and get them to do something for one of your constituents and then they come back up here on an appropriation, human nature being what it is, there is going to be an influence there passing back and forth. . . . I have seen it happen many, many times in my experience here, and I know it does happen all the time." (*Organization of Congress: Hearings before the Joint Committee,* 79th Cong., 1st sess., p. 297.)

zen groups like the United Nations Association or the Foreign Policy Association can scarcely match in potency even one important local of the Farm Bureau Federation, the CIO, or the National Association of Manufacturers. The State Department, moreover, is a small department; its personnel is recruited almost wholly on a career basis; it has little patronage to dispense. Aside from an occasional ambassadorship, which is too important and too infrequent a plum to waste on Congressmen, there is little help the individual Congressman can get in strengthening his organization back home. Worse yet, for a variety of reasons, Foreign Service personnel until recently has been recruited in significant part from social, educational, and economic strata that many members of Congress distrust. A distinguished young Congressman of intelligence and balance remarks: "The State Department is an old class bureaucracy based on seniority, protocol, and everything else of that kind." [5] The myth may be false, but it persists (although, as we shall see in a moment, the Foreign Service is sometimes an asset).

There are other, more irrational factors, on the debit side of the Department's balance sheet. The State Department is by the very nature of its function a "troublemaker" for Congress in the present state of the world. It can rarely bring a happy word—a budget surplus, a decrease in expenditures, a spectacular solution to a pressing problem. More often it must demand increased expenditures in election years; it proposes policies that require a large military establishment and a draft; it presents the Congress with issues from which a Congressman can gain few votes but which he cannot successfully dodge. It would be interesting to speculate on the hatreds that were projected by Congressmen on the State Department in 1948 as a result of having to appropriate six billion for foreign relief and pass a peacetime draft act, both in an election year.

Moreover, desire to locate guilt for the state of the world leads directly to the door of the Department that is "responsible" for that condition. If foreign relief and a peacetime draft are necessary,

---

[5] Conversation with the writer. For evidence of a contrary view, see Representative Stefan's comments, footnote 3. . . .

it is easy to believe that the State Department has bungled. If the Department operated more effectively, one would like to believe, the country would not be faced with its great crisis in Soviet-American relations.

The State Department therefore meets a much more hostile and distrustful Congress than do most other departments. Congressional distrust is revealed by such items as its initial refusal to allow complete State Department operation of the Voice of America programs, and perhaps even more clearly, by the establishment of a separate agency for the administration of the European Recovery Program. One has only to spend a few days on Capitol Hill to realize how widespread is Congressional distrust and resentment of the Department of State.

MANIPULATING THE PICTURE OF REALITY

The real power of the executive-administrative in playing the game of politics with Congress cannot rest on the old-fashioned techniques of the ward leader. Nor does it need to. For the trump card of the executive-administrative in foreign affairs is not its capacity for influencing the Congressman's preferences by ward-heeling methods. Rather, it is the capacity for influencing the Congressman's picture of international reality. This it does in two ways.

First, the Department of State has in the Foreign Service an elite corps whose assertions about international reality may sometimes be highly influential. For despite the hostility of some members toward the stereotype of the "striped pants cookie-pusher," the Foreign Service—perhaps the most group-conscious guild in the federal government—does have some influential allies in Congress. The authors of a recent detailed study of the Foreign Service Act of 1946 remark:

During the course of the eight hearings in executive session before the Subcommittee [of the House Foreign Affairs Committee] . . . a spirit of camaraderie developed between the Foreign Service representatives and the Subcommittee members. There was some social intercourse between the Foreign Service officers, especially Chapin [director of the

Foreign Service] and Harrington [deputy director], and the congressmen. As the bill became more and more "their bill," the Subcommittee members seem to have adopted a rather paternal attitude toward the Foreign Service; the Service became for them somewhat like a constituent, whose rights and interests deserve Congressional protection.[6]

As an elite corps almost wholly insulated from the crasser political influences and completely untainted by charges or innuendo about "party politics," as a guild whose members are carefully recruited according to standards until quite recently severe for the federal government, the Foreign Service evidently appears to some Congressmen as a model of what the civil service ought to be. Testimony from a member of the Foreign Service at times may be extraordinarily influential; Congressmen may be inclined to take Foreign Service views on faith and not subject them to the critical scrutiny they need.[7]

Second, . . . the fact that the executive-administrative as a whole appears to possess a superior claim to information about, and expert interpretation of, international politics does give the President and State Department a certain lever on Congress as on the electorate. For just as the executive-administrative can, within limits, deliberately and systematically shape public opinion by giving different emphasis and interpretation to events, so too can it influence Congressional opinion by the same techniques.[8] More-

[6] Committee on Public Administration Cases, *The Foreign Service Act of 1946*, pp. 112–13.

[7] Thus in connection with the Foreign Service Act of 1946, Mr. Vorys, the chairman of the Congressional subcommittee, asked if the Board of Foreign Service Examiners "were not the cornerstone of the whole Foreign Service personnel system, and was told [by members of the Foreign Service] that it was. On learning this, he said, 'put it in the book,' [i.e., the statute] and the others agreed." Yet the Bureau of the Budget had serious doubts that the board should be given statutory status, and would have challenged the statement that it was in any sense the "cornerstone" of the system. (*Ibid.*, p. 112.)

[8] William L. Neumann (*loc. cit.*) gives a critical evaluation of the Department's use of various "sales techniques" in selling Congress on Administration foreign policy in the postwar years.

over, the growth of the Central Intelligence Agency may over the long run give the executive-administrative enormously better information, and better evaluation of information, than it has ever had before.

It is difficult to evaluate the effectiveness and potentiality of these powers. But the theoretical possibilities contained in the development of a great disproportion between executive, Congress, and electorate in access to information may be imagined by the following mental experiment: Suppose the Chief Executive and his aides were to decide that a preventive war had become indispensable to national survival. Suppose the Congress and the electorate did not share this view. Suppose, finally, that the President and his aides appeared at a hastily summoned, closed meeting of Congress and informed it that Russian war planes were about to begin winging their way to the United States with quantities of atomic bombs. What would Congress do? Indeed, what *could* Congress do?

THE CONSTITUTIONAL DICTATOR IN A MASS SOCIETY

It is at least possible that these techniques for manipulating Congress and public opinion might, under the proper circumstances, transmute presidential supremacy into a peculiarly American form of modern dictatorship. Indeed, our analysis suggests that only some such development will provide the necessary guarantees that the President will be supreme in foreign affairs and untrammeled by "interference" from the national legislature.

Modern society in an age of acute crisis provides fertile soil for such a growth. The onerous burden of freedom, the imperious desires of leadership groups for domination, the crucial need for a "right" decision that will promote security and relieve anxiety— these are some of the preconditions for a flight into authoritarianism.

In the blatant form practiced in the Third Reich or the U.S.S.R., most of us easily recognize that the mass of the people is exploited to satisfy the preferences of the leadership. But the growing discrepancy between the capacities of the electorate and those of certain leadership groups may lead in democratic societies to pressures of a more subtle kind.[9] The universal impulse of the leaders to guide the mass to the "right" policy conclusions is easily converted into a desire to short-circuit the democratic process, particularly, as in foreign policy, when the "right" choice may seem to be a precondition of national survival. The leadership feels that it knows "what the realities of the situation demand." Yet it must submit its policies to the electorate for approval or rejection, even though the irrationalities of the political process may lead to a "wrong" choice —which is to say, to policies that do not secure the preferences of the leadership. The leaders, moreover, may be fortified by the easy conviction that their ends and purposes embody the real preferences of the electorate—preferences obscured by the operation of the political process.

Perhaps, despite these hesitancies, the democratic game must be played out according to the accepted ground rules. The wish to by-pass the rules runs afoul of a deeply rooted institutional framework, reinforced by a powerful body of habitual activities and beliefs. It also runs counter to the tremendous inheritance of democratic slogans, myths, and practices that have surrounded political and administrative leadership from infancy, and which inhibit a conscious declaration or even realization of one's anti-democratic purposes. These conflicting desires of the leadership might perhaps be reconciled if only the citizens could be guided to a "right" decision by surrounding them with the "correct" information, or by withholding intelligence reports adverse to the policy, or by repeating and dramatizing the appropriate symbols. Thus the illusion of freedom and democracy might be maintained; the electorate might continue to believe that it was enforcing its preferences on the leaders; while in reality the leadership would be enforcing its preferences on the electorate.

Unattractive as this picture may appear when drawn so starkly,

[9] For a discussion of some of the social and political consequences of a "disproportionate development of human faculties," see Karl Mannheim, *Man and Society in an Age of Reconstruction* (London, 1940), p. 42.

its appeal must not be underrated.[10] For it would simultaneously satisfy the power needs of driving, aggressive and perhaps charismatic leadership, the desire of followers to be relieved of the responsibility for making burdensome choices, and the verbal and institutional apparatus of democracy. Of all the alternatives, moreover, it may be the easiest to achieve in a crisis world.

ANOTHER WAY OUT

Presidential supremacy—even some form of constitutional dictatorship—*may* be the wave of the future. But if so, then the future lies with values other than rationality, responsibility, and agreement. The central argument of this book is that another way out is still open to us. What is this way?

We must begin with the assumption that discretion over foreign policy by political leadership—often very great discretion—is an ineluctable requirement of survival in modern international politics. [We have contended that] foreign policy is too complicated an affair to be conducted by plebiscite. The basic question is not *whether* political leadership is to exercise discretion in foreign affairs, but *how*. Or put in another way, the question is: What can we do to make it reasonably probable that in exercising its discretion political leadership will maximize—so far as is possible in the kind of world we live in—the values of responsibility, rationality, and agreement?

The argument here is: First, that Congress can be converted into a basic institution for deciding what and whose preferences are to guide the conduct of foreign affairs. There are, however, many obstacles to such a conversion, and these must be removed.

[10] Both as a member of the administrative branch and as an outside observer, the author has been impressed time and again by the extent to which conscientious and socially minded experts can develop unconscious hostilities to democratic politics as a result of their experience in the administrative branch. Deeply devoted to democracy at the verbal level, after a few years in the administrative branch they come to distrust the political processes of democracy and particularly the legislative process, because of the unremitting threat offered by "politics" to the prosecution of "right" policies allegedly beneficial to the electorate.

Second, that the executive-administrative will probably remain the basic institution for interpreting international reality and formulating proposals for dealing with that reality. But if Congress is to perform competently in mediating between preferences and reality, it must develop techniques for more rational evaluation of executive-administrative reports and policy proposals.

Third, that these developments in themselves will greatly facilitate the process of making foreign policy on the basis of the widest possible agreement. There are, to be sure, some potential conflicts between the goals of rationality and responsibility on the one side, and the goal of agreement on the other. To some extent, however, these conflicts can be resolved.

.　.　.　.　.

Responsibility, Confidence, Collaboration

The stark principle of separation of powers is suspicion: suspicion of the President by Congress, of Congress by the President, of both by the electorate. Because the President suspects the aims and competence of Congress he tries when possible to conduct foreign policy by drawing upon his indefinable reservoir of inherent powers; because Congress suspects the aims and competence of the President, it sews him when it can into a legislative strait-jacket.

THE CONCEPT OF CONFIDENCE

The opposing principle is confidence. In a broad political sense, confidence is my expectation that X will act in a manner suitable to my preferences—combined, perhaps, with the reservation that I will catch him if he does not. If I have great confidence in X, I shall probably grant him great discretion if he seems to need it, for I anticipate that he will act as I would act if I understood the details of the situation as well as he. But I will not have confidence in X if I doubt his competence; this, essentially, is why the executive-administrative distrusts Congress on matters of foreign policy. Nor will I have confidence in X if I doubt that he genuinely accepts my preferences; this, essentially, is why Congress distrusts the executive-administrative on matters of foreign policy.

American observers of English political institutions have sometimes misread the nature of "confidence" in the relationship between Cabinet and Commons. They have taken for the essence of the relationship the formal sanctions that may ultimately be employed to bring about a government based on "confidence"—the vote of "no confidence" by Commons, dissolution by the Crown. Some observers, like Thomas K. Finletter, would therefore go so far as to import the right of dissolution into the American Constitution.[11]

But we do not need to import the British constitution in order to develop something approaching a condition of "confidence" in the American political system. To be sure, the British constitution produces the relationship with an automaticity that in all likelihood will never be achieved in this country. Yet even there, it is vital to remember, for over half a century no cabinet that began life with its party in control of the House has fallen because of a vote of no confidence.

The active and vital institutions that have made the fall of a cabinet unlikely are the parties. For the Prime Minister and his colleagues hold their positions only because they are the acknowledged and accepted leaders of their party; because they are elected by the parliamentary party and are responsive to it; and because members of the party in the House of Commons have the well-founded expectation that their party leaders will, as a matter of course, follow the set of preferences defined by the party program and the decisions of the annual party conferences. And when a party leader is not responsive to the parliamentary party or annual conference he will, like Ramsay MacDonald, be scuttled as head of the party.

There are, in my view, three key pre-conditions for developing a relationship of "confidence" between executive and Congress under the American system. . . . The first pre-condition is the development of techniques for improving Congressional competence

[11] *Can Representative Government Do the Job?* (Reynal & Hitchcock, 1945).

in foreign affairs. The President is unlikely to forego using his inherent powers so long as he has a profound distrust of Congressional competence in the delicate field of foreign policy. . . .

The second pre-condition is a greater measure of party responsibility. The President must have the confidence of his own party. He and his party in Congress must work together as a part of a team, enforcing responsibility on the President himself, on the administrative branch, and not least on party members in Congress. . . .

The third pre-condition is implied by the other two; executive and Congress must collaborate in the formulation of basic foreign policies.[12]

COLLABORATION: A CASE HISTORY

As a technique for overcoming the internal stresses produced by the American constitutional system, consultation between policymakers in the executive and in Congress has been suggested by many a Secretary of State and many a Senator. From time to time Secretaries of State have, like Hay and Root, made a practice of conferring with leading Senators in advance of treaty negotiations. The practice of sending Congressional leaders as delegates to international conferences has been used sporadically since the War of 1812.

But the real development of systematic and extensive collaboration between executive and Congress on foreign policy dates only from 1943. As much as anything, this development was a product of the traumatic experience of Wilson's overwhelming defeat at the hands of Senator Lodge. Franklin Roosevelt and Cordell Hull, the one in the executive branch at the time, the other in Congress, had witnessed the destruction of what both men enthusiastically believed was a heroic figure and a hope for the world—Wilson and the League. A generation later the potential parallel was too pat to be missed. Was a new League sponsored by the executive to suffer at

---

[12] Cf. Edwin S. Corwin, *The President: Office and Powers,* 3d ed. (New York University Press, 1948), pp. 270–71.

the hands of the Senate the same fate as the old? It seemed clear that if the Wilson-Lodge battle were not to be repeated, it would be wise for executive and Congress to strike up an alliance. The United Nations Charter therefore became the first real testing ground for executive-Congressional collaboration and, at the same time, for bipartisan collaboration.

Sensitized to Congressional attitudes by his long legislative experience and many close friendships with Senators and Representatives, Secretary Hull from the beginning had attempted to maintain good working relations with the Congress. He frequently appeared before Congressional committees, attended group conferences with Congressmen, cautioned his assistants about their sometimes hostile attitudes toward Congress, and occasionally restrained their desires to join in open battle.

In 1943, therefore, when it seemed that time was ripening for action on an international organization, the Secretary and his assistants co-operated cautiously with members of Congress interested in promoting various resolutions favorable to such a policy. In March of that year the Department prepared a brief resolution of its own, and a few days later the Secretary conferred with the Minority Leader, Senator McNary, and a bipartisan group of four men from the Foreign Relations Committee—Senators Connally, George, Vandenberg, and Gillette. Soon thereafter he had a meeting with the so-called B_2H_2 group—Senators Ball, Burton, Hatch, and Hill—which was actively working for American membership in an international organization. In the House, where Representative Fulbright had introduced a favorable resolution, the Secretary kept in touch with Chairman Bloom of the Foreign Affairs Committee and with the Speaker, who in turn had been negotiating with majority and minority members sympathetic to an "internationalist" policy.

During the summer recess, ten Congressional teams, each consisting of a member of the Senate and the House, took the stump throughout the country and discussed the B_2H_2 resolution. Both the House and the Senate passed favorable resolutions that fall. And not long afterward, immediately following the Moscow conference where agreement had been formally obtained for a postwar international security organization, the Secretary of State, for the first time in history, addressed the two houses in joint session.

Meanwhile, the Department had been making studies and finally tentative drafts of the charter of an international organization to which the United States might adhere. During this preparation and drafting, a number of conferences had been held with leading members of the Senate and House foreign affairs committees, at which their views were carefully solicited and those of the State Department were made known. By March of 1944 preparations had reached a stage where the Secretary and the foreign affairs committees thought it desirable to designate certain members to maintain liaison with the Secretary and the Department. Four Democratic and four Republican members were named to this special subcommittee, which met with the Secretary about once every ten days and exchanged views on the proposed charter. The Secretary also held meetings with House leaders of both parties and with the now widely known B_2H_2 quadrumvirate.

At the Dumbarton Oaks conference in late summer of 1944, the draft thus worked out by consultation was presented to the British, Russians, and Chinese. Although there were no Congressional members in the American delegation, the Congressional leaders knew in advance what the American proposals were to be; moreover, the Secretary continued his conferences throughout this period with the members of the Foreign Relations Committee, the B_2H_2 group, and the House leadership.

After the conference was ended, the meetings were concluded; and apparently Mr. Hull's resignation after the elections led to a decline in collaboration. But following the Yalta conference, on the President's instructions the new Secretary, Mr. Stettinius, appointed Senators Vandenberg and Connally as delegates to the San Francisco Conference which prepared the final draft of the United Nations Charter.[13]

[13] For these details, see Cordell Hull, *Memoirs* (Macmillan, 1948), I, 214–15; II, 1312–14, 1657–98; Lawrence H. Chamberlain and Richard C. Snyder,

Since that time, the practice of consultation and collaboration has become rather common—Greek-Turkish aid, European recovery, North Atlantic Pact, for example—but by no means customary. Policies regarding German and Japanese occupation, Palestine, and, above all, China have evidently been entirely executive in nature; and there seems to have been no prior consultation with Congressional leaders on the terms of the 1949 bill for sending arms to Europe.

What are some of the lessons of the experiments in consultation so far?

SOME GUIDES FOR THE FUTURE

Despite these beginnings, collaboration need not mean bipartisanship. The one experiment has been so completely enmeshed in the other that it is easy to confuse the two. Yet this is an unfortunate identification. For there are issues of foreign policy on which the parties are bound to take opposing stands; and this should not prevent collaboration between the President and his own party members in Congress.

Collaboration means co-operation in the making of policy between policy-makers in the executive-administrative, and the relevant "policy specialists" in Congress. The range of co-operative activities may extend from intimate collaboration in the detailed formulation of policy to merely informative consultation when the Secretary meets with Congressional policy specialists to exchange information and views. American participation in the United Nations came about as a result of the first, as we have just seen. The second was frequently employed during the "Berlin crisis" in 1948 and 1949, when the Secretary of State consulted with the leaders of the Senate and House foreign affairs committees, informed them of the line the United States was prepared to take, and received their public support. Greek-Turkish aid and the European Recovery Program fell somewhere in between. The North Atlantic Pact

---

American Foreign Policy (Rinehart, 1948), p. 113; James Byrnes, *Speaking Frankly* (Harper, 1947), p. 234.

was closer to the pattern of collaboration on the United Nations Charter.

Collaboration is vital to "confidence" because it provides Congress with some surety that its preferences will be taken into account. The Congressional policy specialist is an intermediary in whom the Congressman believes he can repose some trust. Thus Congressman Monroney said of the Bretton Woods proposals:

I think our Banking and Currency Committee has finished one of the hardest bills our committee has ever handled—Bretton Woods. The only thing that saved it and resulted in passage with only eighteen opposition votes against it [in the House] was the fact that Jesse Wolcott, the Republican ranking member, and Mr. Spence [the Democratic committee chairman] had participated in Bretton Woods, and practically everything had been presented to them as they went along.[14]

There are, however, a number of pitfalls that are not easy to avoid. First, there are all the ordinary problems of people working together, problems magnified in this case by the tradition of separation of powers. Tradition sanctifies the belief that conflict between the executive and Congress is in some mysterious way a genuine benefit. Even such a shrewd participant-observer as Robert Luce succumbed to the *mystique* of separation of powers. Arguing from the dubious axiom of social Darwinism that "wise progress comes from conflict," he urged that on the whole more good than harm issued from "the perpetual struggle between Congress and the President. . . ." [15] In a war in which the executive is the enemy, a man's reputation and influence are at stake if he insists upon looking at the executive as an ally. When Senator Pittman was chairman of the Foreign Relations Committee he opposed active collaboration with the State Department because, he said, it would reduce his effectiveness in the Senate.[16] One cannot serve two masters.

[14] *Organization of Congress: Hearings before the Joint Committee,* 79th Cong., 1st sess., Part V, p. 1169.
[15] *Legislative Problems* (Houghton Mifflin, 1935), p. 239.
[16] Hull, *op. cit.,* I, 216.

Collaboration, too, is irksome, time-consuming, tiring—which is, presumably, why Secretary Byrnes, even after his lengthy experience in the Senate, began his secretaryship by ignoring his ex-colleagues on the Foreign Relations Committee.[17] And then there are the interminable vexing limitations of human personalities. Jealousies, hatreds, status, protocol—all must be taken into account.

This means that no purely mechanical arrangements will automatically make for effective collaboration. Judgment, tact, and wisdom in the ways of human beings cannot be eliminated as vital elements in the structure of confidence. Precisely for the same reasons that the relationship between a President and his cabinet cannot be fixed by rules, the relationship between the policy specialists on the Foreign Relations Committee, the Secretary of State, and the President cannot be tightly prescribed.

Second, many difficulties are certain to stem from the fact that it is both desirable and yet impossible to distinguish between policy and administration, between collaboration on policy and "interference" in administration. There is a point at which Congressional collaboration might become "interference" of a kind destructive to effective organization, morale, discipline, and action. As Secretary Acheson has said: "We do not want to put the secretaryship of State in a commission." [18]

International events will not conveniently gear themselves to the cogwheel of Congressional routine. Decisions must be made. Day-to-day activities must go on. In case of disagreement, someone must ultimately take the responsibility for decision. Members of the State Department ought not to have to choose between obeying the Secretary or obeying a Congressional leader. Responsibility is possible only if it is clearly understood that internally the Department is responsible only to the Secretary, and that the Secretary in turn is fully responsible for what goes on in the Department.

[17] Joseph and Stewart Alsop, "Chairman Vandenberg of the Senate Foreign Relations Committee" in Chamberlain and Snyder, *op. cit.*, p. 131.
[18] *Org. of Cong., Hearings,* p. 509.

No one, perhaps, has put the case more strongly than Senator Vandenberg in defining the limits of bipartisan consultation:

When and where it is possible, in clearly channeled and clearly identified projects, for the legislature, the Executive, and the two major parties to proceed from the beginning to the end of a specific adventure, so that all are consulted in respect to all phases of the undertaking, I think it is a tremendously useful thing. . . . But to think that that can be done as an every-day practice in regard to all of the multiple problems of international import which now descend upon the State Department every day, in my opinion is totally out of the question.[19]

If our analysis is correct, however, the practice of consultation itself—particularly if combined with a responsible party system—will help to keep Congressional action at the level of high policy rather than of departmental details. For Congress will insist on control over details only so long as it lacks confidence in the executive-administrative.[20] Collaboration and party responsibility will help to create that confidence and will thereby permit Congressional leadership to concentrate on the formulation of basic policy.

The third difficulty is the converse of the second: a façade of collaboration may be set up to conceal the fact that policy is made entirely by the executive-administrative. Unless the Congressional policy specialists are somewhere near the level of competence of the Secretary of State and his top advisers, collaboration may not do much more than provide a disguised transmission belt for carrying State Department policies into Congress. Almost no one outside the Foreign Relations Committee and the Secretary can know

[19] *Congressional Record,* June 11, 1948, p. 7800.
[20] I speak here of Congress as a body. Individual Congressmen like Representative May will no doubt seek to influence individual administrators. But party discipline will greatly reduce their power. The administrator will feel more independent of individual Congressmen and more dependent on Congress as a body.

when, or whether, this occurs. For the decisive relationship exists in the closed meetings between Secretary and Congressional policy specialists. That is the moment when Secretary and, say, chairman of Foreign Relations meet as equals in a give-and-take relationship, or as unequals in which the Secretary gives and the chairman takes.

Much must necessarily depend upon the personalities and competence of the two men and the men around each, and a great variety of relationships must be anticipated. But so far as formal organization may help, despite the personalities involved, a great deal will depend upon the capacity of Congress for securing independent information and policy analysis. So long as Congress lacks these, it is almost inevitable that the Secretary will always be armed with better information and more sophisticated policy analysis, against which the stubbornness or mere common sense of the Congressional policy specialist will not easily prevail.

The Congressman may, of course, urge his superior understanding of Congressional opinion against a proposed policy, and such urgings may well be effective. But it must not be forgotten that the role of the policy specialist in Congress is such that if you persuade him of the correctness of the policy, you persuade a good share of the Congress too. It is not improbable that, since the war, to secure the support of Senators Vandenberg and Connally for a policy was all but to secure the support of a majority of the Senate and House. It is precisely because of the influential position of the policy specialist that the techniques necessary for raising the level of Congressional competence are an indispensable prerequisite to effective Congressional collaboration.

The fourth difficulty is a product of the third. There is always the possibility that when collaboration is combined with bipartisanship, the opposition may have its head lopped off—or its brains blown out. For, in the Senate at least, there is not likely to be anyone in the minority party who will speak with the authority or competence of the ranking minority members of the Foreign Relations Committee. Capture them, and the opposition is likely to be silenced or, worse yet, silly. It is difficult to read the Senate debates on the North Atlantic Treaty without feeling that whatever case the opponents may have had, they seemed quite incapable of making it.

I am not arguing that opposition is in some mysterious way desirable in itself, nor that bipartisanship is for that reason bad. But rational choices cannot be made unless the alternatives are intelligently presented, and bipartisan collaboration may sometimes prevent the intelligent presentation of alternatives. . . .

ACCOUNTABILITY OF EXECUTIVE PERSONNEL

In the summer of 1949 the question of confidence came up in the Senate in connection with the nomination as Assistant Secretary for Far Eastern Affairs of Mr. W. Walton Butterworth, a Foreign Service officer who had been Director of the Office of Far Eastern Affairs. Mr. Butterworth had been in charge of Far Eastern policy during the period of Nationalist defeat and Communist victory in China. Throughout this period that policy had always been made by a relatively small group.[21] Congressional leaders had not been consulted. The Wedemeyer report, which was known to offer an alternative policy to that of the State Department, had been suppressed by President and State Department. With the crumbling of the Nationalists there was widespread discontent in Congress over our China policy. At one peak of this discontent Mr. Butterworth's nomination was submitted for Senatorial approval.

Although the Foreign Relations Committee gave a favorable report, on the floor of the Senate it came out that Senator Vandenberg, the ranking minority member of the Committee, had simply voted "present." In the indirect Senatorial style he likes to employ, Senator Vandenberg stated his reasons:

> The senior Senator from Michigan did not want to vote against Mr. Butterworth because he considered that he is one of the most distinguished and able career men in the career service, and that in his relationship to the far eastern question he is not the responsible actor in the drama. . . . On the other hand, the senior Senator from Michigan thought it was a very great mistake in public policy, in the appoint-

[21] Joseph Alsop (New York *Herald Tribune,* May 23, 1949, p. 21) describes the principal actors in some detail.

ment of a new Assistant Secretary in charge of far eastern affairs in general, and in China in particular, not to bring a fresh point of view to the assignment, rather than simply to continue the regime which, for one reason or another, is inevitably connected with a very tragic failure of our policies in the Far East.[22]

Senator Brewster urged that the appointment should perhaps be turned down as a vote of no confidence in the China policy.

Now, observing the evolution of the parliamentary process and observing the functioning of it under the parliamentary system in Britain and in other countries, is it not perhaps appropriate that in the promotion of men in the State Department considerations such as the Senator from Michigan suggests may properly be taken into account, and that, in this instance, with full understanding that we are not reflecting upon the individual, and are not challenging his loyalty or devotion, or even his competency, he is so closely identified with what has seemed to be a tragic failure, that it would not be wise and in the public interest that he should at this time receive recognition of that character?

Unless we are to move in that direction I see no indication that the administration, as now constituted, are likely to give our views here the consideration which seems to me to be essential if their policies are to command the confidence of the country as a whole.[23]

Senator Brewster evidently had in mind the fact that under the parliamentary system in England, it is not unusual for an individual minister to resign when he has lost the confidence of a House of Commons that, however, still retains confidence in the cabinet as a whole.[24] Thus in 1935, when the Hoare–Laval pact on Ethiopia was met with a wave of popular and parliamentary revulsion, the foreign minister, Sir Samuel Hoare, resigned, saying to the House:

[22] *Congressional Record,* June 24, 1949, p. 8292.
[23] *Ibid.,* p. 8293.
[24] Instances are cited in W. Ivor Jennings, *Cabinet Government,* rev. ed. (Cambridge University Press), 1950, pp. 461–63.

There is the hard ineluctable fact that I have not got the confidence of the great body of opinion in the country, and I feel that it is essential for the Foreign Secretary, more than any other Minister in the country, to have behind him the general approval of his fellow-countrymen. I have not got that general approval behind me to-day, and as soon as I realised that fact . . . I asked the Prime Minister to accept my resignation.[25]

Is something like this practice desirable in the United States as an extension of the principle of "confidence"? The answer is decisively in the affirmative. There are occasions on which it might be desirable for Congress to debate a vote of confidence, or no confidence, as a means of indicating to the executive-administrative what Congressional opinion is with respect to some foreign policy or some responsible official. There are, nevertheless, certain vital considerations to be kept in mind.

For one thing, it is desirable to maintain a distinction whenever possible between political officials and professional civil servants. The great difficulty in the Butterworth case, as both Senator Vandenberg and Senator Brewster saw, was that a refusal to confirm the nomination would constitute a decisive blow to a career officer. Yet they were simultaneously frustrated by the absence of any "political" official whom they could hold accountable, and the plain fact that an official at the assistant secretary level is an important policy-maker whose preferences and reality views are bound to shape foreign policy. The position is highly "political" in nature, and yet one requiring the kind of expertness that can normally be expected only from a career official.

Here is another point where the values of rationality seem to conflict with the values of responsibility. To say that the position should be filled by a political appointee is to sacrifice professional competence to political responsibility; but to say that the position should be filled by a career officer who cannot be criticized on political grounds is to sacrifice responsibility to professional competence.

[25] Quoted in Jennings, *op. cit.*, p. 444.

If the claims of competence demand that the opportunities of the career service be expanded upward, the claims of responsibility insist that the accountability and influence of the political official be expanded downward. If the private preferences of career officers are not to establish the nation's foreign policies, a greater role must be allotted to the political official, that is, to the man whose primary task is to see that the appropriate preferences are taken into account. This may well require an increase in the number of political officials operating at the level of the secretary's office. And though in doing so there are very real dangers of creating a top-heavy organization, it seems doubtful that these are as great as the dangers flowing out of our growing enthusiasm for pushing career servants upward to policy-making positions where they are presumed to be above criticism.

Second, a vote of no confidence in an individual ought to be distinguished from a vote of no confidence in a policy. It is possible that Senator Brewster was not only aiming his shot at the wrong target, but he was using the wrong weapon. Unless the issue is clearly a question of confidence in an individual, the appropriate weapon would seem to be a concurrent resolution criticizing or supporting a given policy. It was, after all, the entire China policy that was subject to criticism.

Suggestions for Further Reading

BAILEY, STEPHEN K., *Congress Makes a Law* (New York: Columbia University Press, 1950).

BOLLING, RICHARD, *House Out of Order* (New York: Dutton, 1965).

BURNS, JAMES MACGREGOR, *Deadlock of Democracy: Four-Party Politics in America* (Englewood Cliffs, N.J.: Prentice-Hall, 1963).

CATER, DOUGLAS, *Power in Washington* (New York: Random House, 1964).

CLAPP, CHARLES E., *The Congressman: His Work as He Sees It* (Washington, D.C.: The Brookings Institution, 1963).

DAVIDSON, ROGER, DAVID KOVENOCK, and MICHAEL O'LEARY, *Congress in Crisis: Politics and Congressional Reform* (Belmont, Calif.: Wadsworth Publishing Co., 1966).

DE GRAZIA, ALFRED, ed., *Congress: The First Branch of Government* (Washington, D.C.: American Enterprise Institute, 1966).

ENGLER, ROBERT, *The Politics of Oil* (New York: The Macmillan Co., 1961).

FENNO, RICHARD F., JR., *The Power of the Purse* (Boston: Little, Brown, 1966).

227

228 STUDIES ON CONGRESS

GALLOWAY, GEORGE B., *The Legislative Process in Congress* (New York: Thomas Y. Crowell, 1953).

GRIFFITH, ERNEST S., *Congress: Its Contemporary Role,* Third Edition (New York: New York University Press, 1961).

JONES, CHARLES O., *Party and Policy Making: The House Republican Policy Committee* (New Brunswick, N.J.: Rutgers University Press, 1965).

LATHAM, EARL, *The Group Basis of Politics* (Ithaca: Cornell University Press, 1952).

MACNEIL, NEIL, *Forge of Democracy* (New York: David McKay, 1963).

MATTHEWS, DONALD R., *U.S. Senators and Their World* (Chapel Hill: University of North Carolina Press, 1960).

MILBRATH, LESTER W., *The Washington Lobbyists* (Chicago: Rand McNally, 1963).

PEABODY, ROBERT L., and NELSON W. POLSBY, *New Perspectives on the House of Representatives* (Chicago: Rand McNally, 1963).

RANNEY, AUSTIN, *The Doctrine of Responsible Party Government* (Urbana: University of Illinois Press, 1962).

RIPLEY, RANDALL B., *Party Leadership in the House of Representatives* (Washington, D.C.: The Brookings Institution, 1967).

ROBINSON, JAMES A., *The House Rules Committee* (Indianapolis and New York: Bobbs-Merrill, 1963).

TRUMAN, DAVID B., ed., *The Congress and America's Future* (Englewood Cliffs, N.J.: Prentice-Hall, 1965).

ZEIGLER, HARMON, *Interest Groups in American Society* (Englewood Cliffs, N.J.: Prentice-Hall, 1963).

The Contributors

JOSEPH S. CLARK is a former United States Senator from Pennsylvania.

PAUL W. CHERINGTON is Professor at the Harvard University Graduate School of Business Administration.

ROBERT A. DAHL is Sterling Professor of Political Science at Yale University.

LEWIS A. FROMAN, JR., is Associate Professor of Political Science at the University of California at Irvine.

RALPH L. GILLEN is a member of the Washington staff of McKinsey and Company.

RALPH K. HUITT is Professor of Political Science at the University of Wisconsin and served as Assistant Secretary for Legislation in the United States Department of Health, Education, and Welfare.

CHARLES O. JONES is Professor of Political Science at the University of Pittsburgh.

CLEM MILLER was a Representative in Congress from the First District of California. He was killed in an airplane accident in 1962.

JEFFREY L. PRESSMAN wrote the book from which the selection in this volume was taken while an undergraduate at Yale University. He is presently at the University of Buffalo.

DATE DUE

DEC 9 74			
JAN 73			
GAYLORD			PRINTED IN U.S.A.